H. G. Wells and Rebecca West

Thus piteously Love closed what he begat:
The union of this ever-diverse pair!
These two were rapid falcons in a snare,
Condemn'd to do the flitting of the bat.
Lovers beneath the singing sky of May,
They wander'd once; clear as the dew on flowers:
But they fed not on the advancing hours:
Their hearts held cravings for the buried day.
Then each applied to each that fatal knife,
Deep questioning, which probes to endless dole.
Ah, what a dusty answer gets the soul
When hot for certainties in this our life!—
In tragic hints here see what evermore
Moves dark as yonder midnight ocean's force,
Thundering like ramping hosts of warrior horse,
To throw that faint thin line upon the shore!

—George Meredith, "Modern Love"

GORDON N. RAY

H.G. Wells & Rebecca West

New Haven: Yale University Press: 1974

102465

Designed by Sally Sullivan
and set in Baskerville type.
Printed in the United States of America by
Vail-Ballou Press, Inc., Binghamton, N.Y.

Distributed in Latin America by Kaiman & Polon, Inc.,
New York City; in Japan by John Weatherhill, Inc., Tokyo.

For Dame Rebecca West
With Profound Gratitude

CONTENTS

ILLUSTRATIONS

Photographs (following page 102)

The Wells family and guests at Easton
Glebe about 1912

Brig-y-don, Victoria Avenue, Hunstanton,
in 1973

Quinbury, Braughing, in 1973

Two views of Easton Glebe about 1915

Ford Madox Ford and Rebecca West about 1914

Ford Madox Ford, Violet Hunt, and H. G. Wells
about 1914

H. G. Wells about 1915

Rebecca and Anthony West about 1916

H. G. Wells at the British Association
meeting, 1923

Rebecca West about 1923

Rebecca and Anthony West about 1928

H. G. Wells at a garden party, King's College,
Cambridge, 1931

Rebecca West about 1932

Sketches by Wells

PREFACE

This book had its beginning in 1970 when Dame Rebecca West allowed me to read more than 800 letters which H. G. Wells had written to her. I first saw these letters in a suitcase where they had been tightly packed many years earlier. Most were undated and not many of their postmarked envelopes had survived, but they appeared to be in layers corresponding to the periods at which they were written. By treating their container as an archaeological dig, I was able with the aid of the internal evidence offered by the letters themselves to arrange them in something like chronological order.

Dame Rebecca's letters to Wells during the ten years that they were together had been destroyed by him long after their separation. Only five have survived (there are eight more of later date), either because he returned them to her with messages added or because she retained drafts. Their destruction is particularly to be regretted. Her replies must have been quite as interesting as the letters that elicited them, and the two sides of the correspondence together would surely have constituted one of the great exchanges of literary history. Yet by supplementing Wells's letters with Dame Rebecca's published writings, which contain much direct or implied autobiography, I was able to go some way towards compensating for this gap in the record.

Then came a great piece of good fortune. During visits which I paid to London in the summers of 1971, 1972, and 1973 (other work left summer as my main time for writing), Dame Rebecca read the successive drafts of my story with the most scrupulous care. She corrected errors of fact, filled in the inevitable omissions of a narrative based on fragmentary materials, and set down with her accustomed force and wit how she herself regarded this part of her life. This collaboration continued, indeed, until my typescript went to the printer. Her candor was absolute. As she approached eighty, she remarked, her "fair fame" was hardly an overriding consideration. "This is a long essay in self-analysis," she wrote to me on one occasion, "which experts say is always self-destructive, so Heaven knows what you will be responsible for." And indeed her reexamination of this critical period of early life must have involved, like Newman's in writing his *Apologia Pro Vita Sua,* "the ripping up of old griefs, and the venturing again upon the *infandum dolorem* of years, in which the stars of this lower heaven were one by one going out." She could never bring herself, for example, to reread the letter which she sent to Wells in the early summer of 1913 after his second rejection of her. I should add. that, though Dame Rebecca has encouraged me to publish my narrative, she does not agree in every instance with my interpretations of fact or my analysis of her writings.

Even with Dame Rebecca's assistance, I have not been able to make up entirely for the imbalance in my materials. The sheer happiness that she and Wells enjoyed in each other's company still does not sufficiently appear. After their first four years together Wells wrote more often than not under the spur of some passing irritation. His letters, as Dame Rebecca put it, often bear witness to both "his need to feel rage and a betraying inability to invent a plausible cause for it," and it is these letters which of necessity dominate the latter part of my narrative. Mindful of this "lethal nagging," Dame Rebecca noted of one of my early drafts that it seemed to present Wells and herself "as a couple of inveterately quarrelsome people who brawled their way through a sexual relationship." This distortion remains, though it is no longer so acute as before.

As a biographer, I found the preparation of this book a salutary experience. In writing my life of Thackeray some years ago, I dealt with a man who had been dead for nearly a century. Having assembled the surviving documents bearing on him, both printed and manuscript, I could proceed with the assurance that I knew at least as much as anyone else could know. If I went wrong, no one could contradict me. This is how one achieves a "definitive biography." In dealing with Wells and Dame Rebecca, on the other hand, I have had the rare opportunity of submitting my story to the scrutiny of one of its principals. The resulting narrative, whatever its other deficiencies, has an authority not to be attained by one based on documents alone. Most biography is indeed, as Voltaire said of history, *une fable convenue.*

10 March 1974   G. N. R.

This is the story of the ten-year love affair of H. G. Wells and Rebecca West, "the woman of my life," as he called her. It began during the spring of 1913 when Wells was forty-six and Rebecca twenty; it ended during the autumn of 1923 when Wells was fifty-six and Rebecca thirty. It is a story, among other things, of time's revenges. In 1913 Wells was for many readers the most exciting writer in English, at the cutting edge of change in a society that called out for such surgery, a vigorous and arresting man. Rebecca was a girl of astonishing talent at the beginning of what seemed sure to be a notable literary career, who was bent on experiencing life with passion. Her love for Wells was such that, after she thought she had lost him, she was reduced to almost suicidal despair. Until their first serious quarrel in 1917, their union, for all its difficulties, was predominantly happy. There followed three years in which a fragile understanding was perilously preserved. From 1920 on, however, their relationship deteriorated rapidly, with Rebecca increasingly anxious to break free and Wells increasingly determined not to let her go. By 1923, though Wells had become world famous, the peak of his accomplishment was in fact behind him, his pleas for a World State were beginning to appear more than a little eccentric, and he was

a tired and sick man on the brink of old age. Rebecca had matured into a strong and brilliant
woman. She was a writer of acknowledged accomplishment, whose desire was no longer for experience but for the peace and quiet that would allow
her to do the work which she knew she had in her.
Now it was Wells who was driven to hysterical attacks
and humiliating appeals in his vain effort to persuade Rebecca that crabbed age and youth *could* live
together.

It is clear enough why Wells was attracted to Rebecca. Women were a necessity to him. He kept the
male friends that he had made in his early years of
struggle, but after success came most of his intimates
were women. He looked to them both for love and
for companionship, and no one in his long life gave
these things to him in the same measure as did Rebecca. When they first met she was a vital and enchanting young girl, but she was also his equal in intellect and personality. He told her early in their life
together: "I loved your clear open hard hitting generous mind first of all and I still love it most of all,
because it is most of you." A tribute he wrote a year
before they separated has the same emphasis: "You
have the most wonderful brain I have ever met, the
sweetest heart, the most loving and delightful humour, wit abounding, on ten thousand occasions you
have been supremely beautiful to me." Their union
was in every sense a full partnership.

Yet there were elements in their relationship
which threatened from the beginning to undermine
it. The complexity of Wells's life during his years
with Rebecca was astonishing. He had three residences: a flat in Whitehall Court, his home at Easton

Glebe in Essex, and whatever out of the way place happened to be Rebecca's current haven—Hunstanton, Braughing, Alderton, or Leigh-on-Sea. For years on end, Rebecca remembered, "he went to Essex on Saturday, reappeared on Monday, left for the flat on Tuesday, and came back to me on Thursday." This febrile and fragmented existence exhausted him and tried his uncertain temper. Moreover, he was driven by a desire to spread his opinions as widely as possible, and he was in constant need of money. In consequence he accepted far too many commissions for newspaper and magazine work. This is a principal reason why his books, which were written in the interstices of these assignments, came more and more to be extempore performances of doubtful literary quality.

Then there was an inherent instability of the triangle to which Wells and Rebecca belonged. Wells had a wife from whom he did not intend to part. In 1894 he had left his first wife, Isabel, to elope with Amy Catherine Robbins. He and "Jane," as Wells called her, had two sons: George ("Gip"), born in 1901, and Frank, born in 1903. Thereafter they ceased to be lovers. It was agreed that Wells should lead his sexual life elsewhere, but without compromising Jane. As he moved from one lady to another during the years that followed, Jane in her ostensible character of deceived wife was the recipient of much sympathy from their friends; but though she feigned ignorance of his affairs, Wells in fact kept her fully informed about them. The innate falseness of this arrangement poisoned Rebecca's life with Wells from its beginning.

Still more basic as a threat to their relationship was

Wells's overmastering determination to leave his mark on his time. Getting his work done was the guiding motive of his mature life, even when it was not clear to him what his work was likely to accomplish. When he and Rebecca were on the verge of separation in 1922, he defined the crucial difference between them in these terms:

> It seems to me that almost fundamental in this trouble is something I should call *Drive.* It's not the same thing as energy because my Drive goes on when I am worked out, producing friction, bad temper, things like this outbreak. It says everlastingly oh *Get on* with it! It is a race against death. It's what you mean when you called me— never mind, we've done with that. It's what I am—I can't help it! You, I don't think, have Drive as I have. Your interest in things, so vivid, so adorable and discursive, so that now you throw light on Spain, on a book, on some poor drab of an unsuccessful actress, on a crime, on riding horses—which I always regarded with scorn and contempt until you took to it—well it's just what the Drive wont permit.

Drive, as Wells explains it here, helps to account for the impact that he made on his age. It helps to account as well for the self-centeredness which is the key to much of his behavior.

Wells was deeply in love with Rebecca, he relied upon her for a kind of companionship that he could get from no one else, but he also quite consciously enlisted her in the service of "drive." Like his earlier mistresses, she had the duty in his eyes of assuaging the physical itch that would otherwise distract him from his writing. In their early years an easy sensuality was a happy aspect of their life together, and Rebecca had no feeling that she was being used as a convenience. But after their first serious quarrel in 1917, Wells's insistence on satisfied desire as a necessity for his work emerged more nakedly. His teasing threat of that year, "I shall make the World State my mistress and love that," no doubt had behind it an awareness of how much simpler his life would be if this expedient were indeed possible. By 1920, when he knew in the back of his mind that he would eventually lose Rebecca, he told her: "I've done good things and big things, . . . [but] righteous self-applause is not happiness. . . . I can't go on being the dull Slave of the Salvage of the World. I can't—in my present state anyhow—bank on religion. God has no thighs and no life." "God has no thighs" is an assertion that would seem ludicrous even from Victor Hugo, yet one should not underestimate the anguish that lies behind it. When it was brought home to Wells in 1924 that Rebecca was permanently gone, he wrote in a rare moment of self-insight that he ought to look for "some sort of body slave" to attend him. Odette Keun, to whom he turned, was far more than this; indeed, she proved in her strange way to be as strong and vivid a personality as Rebecca herself. Yet she too saw clearly enough that she was not at the heart of Wells's life. She wrote to Rebecca in the late 1920s:

> Pidoo [her name for Wells] doesn't really depend on me—I've never known anybody in my

whole life who fundamentally can do without others as he can—it's only a pose of his that he needs people, he only needs them to elaborate his ideas and spread them, and so long as he can work, he'd master every kind of shock, however sorrowful.

Rebecca, like Wells, experienced immense happiness in their ten years together. She found him an enchanting companion, "everything one imagines in the way of genius and fun." They suited each other. Simply to be together, to go out walking, to talk of everything and everybody, was enough for them. In 1914 a common friend told Wells that Rebecca would like "a 5th of you better than the whole life of anyone else," and so she did at first. As time passed, however, she came to see ever more clearly what she was sacrificing.

From the beginning, indeed, their "great adventure" had its sordid side for her. While Wells led an exciting if hectic double life, Rebecca led a boring and difficult single life. The truth of the old cliché, that it is the woman who pays, impressed itself upon her. She found herself confined to a back street, hole-and-corner existence, in which she played a succession of parts that might have been invented by Wilkie Collins for the heroines of his "sensation" novels. For a time she was Mrs. West with Wells as Mr. West and Anthony as their son. Then she became Miss West with Wells as a friend of the family and Anthony as her adopted son or nephew. Even the role of "widow West" was once considered. On trips abroad she was Wells's secretary, Miss West. Each of these roles presented its particular problems. For example, what Thackeray in *Vanity Fair* described as "the Vehmgericht of the Servants' Hall" still had to be endured in the early twentieth century. Servants remained a necessity of life, and Rebecca in her ambiguous position rarely found any that were satisfactory. As she later observed, they were "either dumb clucks who understood nothing, not even the irregularity of the situation, which shows you how stupid they had to be, or impudent sluts, or blackmailers." The result was "sheer domestic discomfort and humiliation."

Then there was the fact of her utter isolation. Initially her sub rosa life with Wells had its element of excitement, but it soon became simply tedious. She was cut off from her accustomed social circle. Her mother altogether disapproved of her liaison, and the friends who remained loyal could not conveniently seek her out in the remote residences where she and Wells successively lived. Between 1914 and 1918 Rebecca saw no one except Wells, her usually hostile servants, and an occasional visitor. Her "dashes" to London did not occur more often than once a month. Even after she moved to her pleasant flat at Queen's Gate Terrace in the winter of 1919/20, her social life remained restricted. Wells was averse to their being publicly "seen in sin." Rarely did they go to the theatre, and on the occasions when they dined out, he usually chose an obscure restaurant in Kensington where they were not likely to be observed.

Most devastating of all to Rebecca was the interruption to her career. The immense promise of her journalistic debut in 1912–1913 was hardly borne out in the ten years that followed. Under the conditions that her life with Wells imposed upon her, she could work only halfheartedly and irregularly. When the Frau Gatternigg episode of 1923 impelled Rebecca to her final break with Wells, she might in view of his recent behavior have thought of him as an elderly, middle class variation on Lord Byron, "mad, bad, and dangerous to know." In fact her loyalty to him never faltered, but neither did her determination to free herself for her work. She had come to regard him as an "arch-muddler" with whom an ordered life was impossible, and she was determined at last to overcome what she had always seen as her "destiny," a "capacity to work well if only I could get some peace, and never to get that peace."

My story deals almost entirely with Wells and Rebecca, yet something should also be said of Jane Wells, of Rebecca's mother, Mrs. Fairfield, and of Anthony, who, though they remain silently in the background, were always in the minds of my two principals. We have seen how Jane pretended ignorance of Wells's life with Rebecca, though she was in fact kept fully informed about it. Appearances thus preserved, she provided Wells with a home where he could live comfortably before the world. As the mistress of Easton Glebe, she seemed the perfect embodiment of the loyal and devoted wife and mother. Moreover, Wells relied on her in many other ways. Though he no doubt made most business decisions himself, he used Jane as his executive secretary in carrying them into effect. When Rebecca, as a device for freeing herself from Wells, pressed him to marry her, he replied that if he divorced Jane, he would find "all his work disorganized—obliged to attend himself to his translation business, his income tax returns, domestic bills, banking accounts."

Jane thus kept intact a home for her two sons and maintained her position in the world as the wife of a great man. She cultivated her own circle of friends, she had her hobbies, and she enjoyed traveling abroad, particularly to Switzerland where she was an enthusiastic skier. Yet she knew that she was no longer at the center of Wells's life. A small, pretty, almost doll-like woman, eager for personal distinction but unable to attain it by the delicate, pastel-like sketches which she wrote, she was no match intellectually or emotionally for Rebecca, and she found herself increasingly shut out from her husband's real interests. Even before this when Wells went into society, he rarely insisted that his wife be invited with him.

Looking back at Jane, one finds it hard to see her as anything but a wistful victim of the way in which Wells ruthlessly adjusted his life to suit his own convenience, a figure who deserves pity and sympathy. But this was not Rebecca's view. She altogether disbelieved in the front that Jane presented to the world and, as time went on, regarded her with more and more fear and suspicion. It was not that Rebecca wanted to replace Jane. "There would have been an honorable way of dealing with the situation," she wrote in 1944, "we could have lived side by side, H. G. was worth that."

Moreover, Rebecca felt that Wells's divided allegiance was tearing him apart. On the one side was Jane, whom Wells wanted to regard as "the wise, calm, and practical good woman of the Proverbs," a

symbol of purity to be revered and cherished, if
usually at a distance. On the other side was Rebecca,
the beloved mistress with whom he passed his most
enjoyable hours, but about whom he could not overcome a feeling of guilt. To the habit of mind implied
by "this sacrifice of the sexual woman to the non-sex-
ual woman," Rebecca attributed the "spinsterishness"
of Wells's treatment of sex in his novels, specifically
in those passages of sentimental rhetoric about his
heroines which she derided in her reviews.

If Jane was Rebecca's villain, Mrs. Fairfield was
Wells's. Rebecca loved her mother with intensity. She
had endured many trials with her during her troubled childhood and indeed had looked after her almost unaided during a serious three-year illness.
However eager Rebecca was to get away from a
home circle which had become gloomy and frustrating, she could not sever her emotional bond to her
mother; however independent she might be in her
judgments, she continued to feel deeply the wound
of her mother's disapproval. It was a heavy burden
to her that from the first Mrs. Fairfield unrelentingly
opposed her affair with Wells.

Wells met Mrs. Fairfield's hostility by a counterat-
tack of his own, though it is not easy to gauge to
what extent he really believed in his indictment of
Rebecca's mother and to what extent he put it forward as a counterbalance to Rebecca's indictment of
Jane. At any rate, he attributed to Mrs. Fairfield a
hatred of men which he saw as the direct consequence of her husband's squandering of his talents
and abandonment of his family. This state of mind
had led her to raise her daughters as dedicated "ca-

reer women." Her success with Rebecca's sisters, Letitia and Winifred, both of whom were soon making good progress in their chosen professions, made all the more bitter her seeming failure with Rebecca, her youngest and most gifted child. In offering this interpretation of her mother's attitude, Wells was at least in line with the epigraph to Rebecca's novel *The Judge*, which is dedicated to Mrs. Fairfield: "Every mother is a judge who sentences the children for the sins of the father."

Wells also found in Mrs. Fairfield's implacable disapproval something more fundamental than distress at the manner in which Rebecca's career had been interrupted. He detected a profound antisexual animus, which had already affected the atmosphere of Rebecca's life at home. Mrs. Fairfield thus became for him an embodiment of unreasoning Puritanism who was constantly endeavoring to poison Rebecca's mind against him as a rake, thereby joining in this category such protesting mothers of earlier mistresses as Mrs. Hubert Bland and Mrs. Pember Reeves. Even after his liaison with Rebecca had achieved permanence, so Wells believed, Mrs. Fairfield continued her campaign to deny them undeserved happiness by urging Rebecca to leave him.

Whatever one may think of these contentions, Wells was surely wrong in a final point of his indictment. He maintained that if Rebecca's mother would only sanction their affair, most of her problems would disappear. No doubt Rebecca's isolation would have been eased by this step towards her "social rehabilitation," but her difficulties with the world in general would hardly have been touched. What

Wells denounced as "Fairfieldism" was in fact the conventional morality of the day. He was mistaking a symptom for a cause.

Anthony West was the third significant figure in the background. None of Wells's earlier love affairs had endured for more than a year or two. Anthony's existence counted for more than any other factor in keeping Wells and Rebecca together long after their union had ceased to be really viable. His birth was not, as has sometimes been suggested, a calculated experiment in eugenics by two of the great intelligences of the age, but rather an inadvertence. Yet he was dearly loved both by Rebecca and by Wells, who did their best to give him a happy childhood. Even after their separation, indeed, their love for him remained so strong as to be the chief cause of disagreement between them. As will be seen, however, there were formidable obstacles to their efforts on Anthony's behalf. Ill nature often showed itself in ways that hurt the child as well as his parents. It was hardly within their power to mitigate his ordeal altogether.

Wells and Rebecca were two extraordinarily gifted and interesting people locked by their profound attachment into an impossible situation. That they remained together for ten years is something of a miracle. Wells's reward was the happiness that Rebecca brought to him during this decade of his life. Rebecca's gain is less clear, but at least it may be said that the things she experienced in these years worked together to make her what she afterwards became. The reader is now invited to follow in detail the successive stages in "the union of this everdiverse pair."

CHAPTER I "Rebecca West"

By 1912 H. G. Wells had reached the high point of his reputation as a serious writer. He had gone from such scientific romances as *The Time Machine* and *The First Men in the Moon* to comic yet moving novels of lower middle class English life like *Kipps* and *The History of Mr. Polly*. Most recently he had undertaken to show his readers how the English social system actually worked in *Tono-Bungay* and *The New Machiavelli*. These imaginative works had been accompanied by volumes of daring speculation on the present ills and future prospects of society, the most important of which were *Mankind in the Making* and *A Modern Utopia*. With the possible exception of Bernard Shaw, no writer in the English-speaking world could rival him as a spokesman for enlightened reform.

Marriage, Wells's novel of that year, was not a major book, but a review of it in the *Freewoman* of 19 September 1912 led to an association which was to be the central fact of his life for more than ten years. In this shrewd and knowledgeable appraisal the re-

1

viewer's chief quarrel with Wells is that he is not serious enough. Though amused by his satirical pictures of his enemies, she finds that they distract the reader from his main theme, the deflection of Trafford's scientific genius from its proper uses in order that his wife Marjorie, "Our Lady of Loot," may be provided with the luxuries of life. "The really fine and encouraging thing about the book is that Mr. Wells sees that Marjorie is a thorough scoundrel. The horror of it is that, confused by her clear eyes and copper hair, he accepts scoundrelism as the normal condition of women." But the reviewer's master stroke was the derision with which she greeted Wells's efforts to depict passion. "He is the Old Maid among novelists," she wrote; "even the sex obsession that lay clotted on 'Ann Veronica' and 'The New Machiavelli' like cold white sauce was merely Old Maids' mania, the reaction towards the flesh of a mind too long absorbed in airships and colloids." [1] This gauntlet was thrown down before the most advanced writer in English, the notorious Don Juan of the intellectuals, whose legendary looseness of conduct, so freely reflected in his novels, caused each new book from his hand to be watched for with bated breath alike by subscribers to the _Spectator_ and leaders of the Fabian Society! It was a way of turning Wells's flank that no one had previously conceived.

"Rebecca West," the author of this review, was then just at the beginning of her notable career. Born Cicily Isabel Fairfield in December 1892, she was one of three daughters in a household (like Bernard Shaw's) of "downstarts." Her father, Charles Fairfield, came from a distinguished Anglo-Irish family, and her mother from a prosperous Edinburgh clan, but they had fallen on evil days. Fairfield's father had been a major in the Coldstream Guards, and he was himself for a time an officer in the Rifle Brigade. But since the family fortune had dwindled to nothing, he was forced to leave the army and take to journalism to support his family. He was a brilliant scholar and writer but also a compulsive gambler whose involvement in one bad risk after another had brought his wife and children to the edge of penury. He finally died, by his own wish altogether alone, in a boarding house at Liverpool, where he was working as a clerk, just as Rebecca was entering on her teens. Yet this handsome, dashing man was as straightforward about ideas as he was devious about money, and in his household "a false statement was pulled up and destroyed like any other intellectual weed." Looking back over these years in her semi-autobiographical novel *The Fountain Overflows*, Rebecca long afterward made her narrator, Rose Aubrey, reflect: "I had a glorious father, I had no father at all."

Rebecca's mother, born Isabella Campbell, was the offspring of a runaway match between a gifted musician and composer named Joseph MacKenzie, who by the time of his early death had become conductor at the Theatre Royal in Edinburgh, and Jessie Watson Campbell, a girl of much higher social standing. There were five children in the family, one of whom later became Sir Alexander MacKenzie, a composer who for many years was principal of the Royal Academy of Music in London. Isabella herself had superb gifts as a pianist, but not being a boy she never re-

ceived proper training. She was a lady of great cul-
tivation, reduced by years of coping with financial disaster to a life of self-sacrificing devotion. To people
unacquainted with her history, she seemed nervous
and odd as well as "thin and wild-looking and badly
dressed."

Rebecca, a bright, eager, impulsive girl, broad-
browed, dark, and striking in appearance, was thus
brought up in a "social vacuum," "not part of any
world." She and her sisters, Letitia (called "Letty")
and Winifred, who were respectively seven and five
years older, had a "troubled quality" which set them
off from other young people, and she was negligent
of her appearance and sometimes uninformed about
the customary patterns of social life. But if she wore
shabby clothes and lived in a broken-down home
with worn-out furnishings, she knew that there was
nothing common or mean about her family. She was
proud of an isolation which confirmed her faith that
music and thinking justly were the important things
in life and which saved her from the insensitivity,
crassness, and ugly possessions of her prosperous acquaintances. It did not disturb her that she made
few friends at school, which she saw as a pointless
"place where nothing happened as it did any where
else," any adherence to whose standards amounted
to "a betrayal of childhood." And so, when Mrs. Aubrey tells Rose and her sisters, "you have had a
dreadful childhood, . . . [but] I think you have quite
enjoyed it," Rose sturdily replies, "Why shouldn't
we? We are not soft." [2]

Much of Rebecca's early life was spent in London
under circumstances of virtual penury similar to

those described in *The Fountain Overflows*. After she
had reached the age of ten, she and her family returned to their native city of Edinburgh. For a time
life passed pleasantly enough for Rebecca, since her
mother was "the most humorous and brave and loving creature" and there were plenty of books in the
house. But after Letitia became a doctor and went to
her first post as an intern, and Winifred departed
for Cheltenham College, Mrs. Fairfield fell ill with
exophthalmic goiter or hyperthyroidism, which for a
time altogether changed her nature, making her irritable and ungrateful. For two years Rebecca had to
put up with her bad temper and in effect administer
the household. Moreover, Rebecca herself, like her
sisters, was subject to a series of tubercular attacks,
which left a lung permanently damaged.

Yet this illness was not an unmixed disaster. During her prolonged recuperation Rebecca became accustomed to "the outdoor exercise and the long
walks that give one fearlessness," and she had leisure
for "the unrestricted desultory reading which is the
proper food for every hungry mind." [3] As she grew
better, she began to see something of life, working
"at various things in various places including a Scottish market garden in the depths of winter." [4] All the
while, she was ambitious to become an actress. Encouraged by the praise of an instructor at the Royal
Academy of Dramatic Arts who had seen her per-
form in Edinburgh, she enrolled in that institution
after she and her mother returned to London in
1908.

These early London years proved to be a time of
trial. Mrs. Fairfield was much better; but Rebecca's

sisters had rejoined the household. Letty was by this time well launched on what was to be a distinguished civil service career, and Winifred trained as a teacher and passed out of the Maria Grey Training College at the top of the list. It was a highly competitive atmosphere and Rebecca searched with great eagerness for a way to leave it, initially by trying to achieve a professional life for herself. The instructor who had been impressed by her acting ability in Edinburgh was no longer at the Royal Academy of Dramatic Arts, however, and after a time the Administrator, Kenneth Barnes, came to the conclusion that Rebecca had "no personality," an extraordinary judgment which he also passed on Carlotta Monterey, who was later to marry Eugene O'Neill. Though Rebecca might still have made an acting career for herself elsewhere, she turned in 1911, when she was still only eighteen, to full-time employment on the staff of the just-founded "weekly feminist review," the *Freewoman*.

Rebecca had taken part in the agitation for women's rights from the age of fourteen, when "she was ragged and worried for wearing a Vote for Women's badge." [5] She was living, as she makes Rose Aubrey reflect, during a "period when feminism was spreading like a forest fire, even in households like ours, where the father vehemently disapproved, and the mother was too busy to consider it, and no propagandist literature entered the home," [6] and after her removal from school she made it her business "to study life from the angle of the Suffrage movement." [7] But there were limits to her militancy. Though as a feminist she regarded herself as living "in a time of war," [8] she admitted, not without a touch of irony, that she was too lazy and nervous to put herself forward as a martyr. She was never imprisoned, she never "hunger struck" (as the phrase then went), and she was never forcibly fed. She attended protest meetings, but she rarely spoke; she took part in demonstrations, but in the rear files. Her role was to observe the movement and to comment on it in print, which she did almost from the time of her first conversion. [9]

The initial number of the *Freewoman,* described by one contributor as "a technical trade journal on Womanhood," appeared under the editorship of Dora Marsden on 23 November 1911. It was written for "freewomen" like Ellen Terry, rather than "bondwomen" who are mere servants to their male masters. From the beginning "Votes for Women" was seen as a relatively unimportant objective; even the sacred Mrs. Pankhurst was chided for her obsession with this subject. The *Freewoman's* attack was on a broader front. Rebecca's first contribution, a routine review of a book on feminism in India, appeared over her real name in the second number. [10] It was not until the issue of 15 February 1912 that she used the name Rebecca West. She had once played this role in *Rosmersholm,* but she attached no symbolic significance to her spur-of-the-moment choice of it as a *nom de plume.* She thought that Cicily Fairfield was an impossible name for a serious writer, suggesting, as it did, "something blond and pretty like Mary Pickford," [11] and she wished to avoid implicating her family in her unrestrained and sometimes hilarious attacks on the enemies of feminism, written from a position of entire emancipation, both moral and intellectual. In this article, for example, she patronized the still celebrated Mrs. Humphry Ward as a belated example of the psychology of the Victorian clergyman class. "Mrs. Ward's gospel is an easy one," she wrote in her final paragraph.

If she were Mrs. Mary A. Ward of Port Matilda, Pa., U.S.A., it would be expressed something like this:—

GIRLS! MAKE LIFE A JOY-RIDE!
BUT DON'T TALK BACK TO THE POLICE!

This easy gospel will give its disciples the heritage one may see in the faces of so many "sheltered women": a smooth brow that has never known the sweat of labour; the lax mouth, flaccid for want of discipline; eyes that blink because they have never seen anything worth looking at; the fat body of the unexercised waster.[12]

In article after article Rebecca went on to demonstrate her wide reading, her fine taste (she was one of D. H. Lawrence's earliest champions), and her nimble wit as well as a knowledge of life and a feeling for its complexities astonishing in a girl of her age. If she also expounded feminist doctrine with an assurance amounting to fanaticism, this was after all what subscribers to the *Freewoman* expected for their three pennies; no doubt she had her private reservations. Her articles soon became the most interesting feature of this otherwise rather shrill and bloodless journal, and there was intense curiosity about this new star in the small firmament of London's advanced intellectuals.

At the time that she first impinged directly on Wells by her review of *Marriage,* Rebecca was as clearly a phenomenon and a portent as he himself had been when he was writing for the *Saturday Review* some seventeen years earlier. In her critical articles there was the same fierce sport with pretenders, the same delight in real achievement. And like Wells in his socialist phase, she too might have been described as "a passion for justice incarnate." The crucible of her early family life, followed by the tempering of five years of varied experience, had given her an insight far beyond her age. Comparing herself with other girls, she could reflect with Rose Aubrey: "They don't have demons in the house, and so long as you can't get rid of them, it gives you a great advantage to know there are such things." [13] A free spirit who had rejected the "gospel of things as they are," [14] she reserved her strongest abhorrence for "the fear of life which is the beginning of all evil." [15] Instead she aspired to a tragic view of the world, which as an artist in words it was her business to express.

Above all, Rebecca was a person who realized life with extraordinary vividness. She wrote in an article of the following year, "I remember when I was seven years old arresting my hoop in full flight on Richmond Green at the discovery that my life was losing colour because I was beginning to think of things not by images but by words." [16] Yet unlike most people, she did not really lose this intensity of awareness as childhood receded. Perhaps the particular note of

her personality is best seen in her description of another little girl of seven, a "wonder-child" whom she
encountered on a train to Canterbury.

> She sat reading a very nice picture-book of the
> Zoo with appalling intensity of interest. A flame
> of vitality played about her, leaving her glowing
> like the boy-satyr in Titian's "Bacchus and
> Ariadne." Her coal-black hair rose strongly
> from her low, broad forehead, and under deep
> brows her eyes brooded with wet, soft fierce-
> ness, like the gaze of an animal. Altogether
> she was rather like a monkey, as many ge-
> niuses—notably Chatterton—have been. About
> all her movements there was a kind of proud
> intelligence, of fiery dignity.
>
> All around her sat aunts, well-fed, well-edu-
> cated, tailor-made women, in whose conversa-
> tion about the dock strike there was more mal-
> ice than stupidity. . . . They evidently had large
> and fixed incomes. They were ugly, not because
> they couldn't help it, but because they despised
> beauty. They belonged to a class that owes its as-
> cendancy to the admiration of the mob for ascet-
> icism. No nun curbing the lusts of the flesh
> could mutilate her ego more than such as these.
> For they have suppressed all sensuous emotions
> and all intellectual passions, and have denied
> themselves all experience in order to cultivate a
> mysterious quality known as "common sense."

Her aunts endeavored to distract the child from her
book with a series of informative remarks on the
passing countryside, but finding it dull in compari-

son with the tigers and anteaters on the pages before her, she at last

> became most properly enraged. She snapped sullenly at her aunts. Immediately they dropped their fatuous benevolence and got nasty. "A very naughty, sulky little girl," they said hatefully, and wagged their heads. The child's eyes blazed through tears, she gulped down sobs that choked her. For about the four hundredth time in her brief existence she wished that she was dead.
>
> It was really a tragic sight. It was so wrong that this fiery being, with her demoniac intensity of feeling, should, at the dawn of her days, have her passion perverted to a hatred of life. . . .
>
> I looked at the wonder-child with deep pity when I got out at Canterbury. She will have a bad time later on.[17]

In this picture of someone very like what she herself had been, both in appearance and in temperament, is to be seen not only the essence of Rebecca's special quality but also her acute awareness of the penalty she had paid and would go on paying for possessing it.

CHAPTER II # *Rebecca Rejected*

Wells was a "Constant Reader" of the *Freewoman* from its inception. Perhaps at the urging of his friend E. S. P. Haynes, a frequent contributor, he sent the magazine an article entitled "Mr. Asquith Will Die" for its third number. In this piece, which he describes as the first from his hand for a specifically feminist publication, he urged the editors to stop attacking the Prime Minister, their current preoccupation.[1] He also wrote for the *Freewoman* on other occasions, though never again at any length, and he was treated by its editors with far more respect than they accorded most public men. Even when his articles for the *Daily Mail* were assailed because they lacked any "preliminary imputation of sin," any acknowledgment of the "fundamental injustice" of society, the anonymous writer (perhaps Rebecca herself, who was by this time Miss Marsden's assistant editor) asked wistfully: "What is the good of being Mr. Wells if one cannot say just what one likes?"[2] Again when Rebecca reviewed a manual of contemporary literature which accused Wells of "timidity in his treatment of the novel," she remarked: "it will take some time to accustom me to an association between timidity and Mr. H. G. Wells." [3]

Wells was prepared, then, to accept Rebecca's review of *Marriage* in a comradely spirit, provocative though it might be, and he promptly asked her to Little Easton Rectory. Miss M. M. Meyer, the Wells's Swiss governess, noted in her diary on 27 September 1912: "Miss Rebecca West arrived to-day. She looks about twenty-two years of age, and is very vivacious. She writes in the *Freewoman* and has just reviewed Mr. Wells's new novel *Marriage*." [4] This was presumably Wells's first opportunity to study Rebecca close at hand. He found a slim, sturdy girl of nineteen, who had nothing of the "eagle look" of her mother and father,[5] but was rather a *brune adorable,* dark both in complexion and hair. The keen intelligence, passionate sympathy, and pungent wit that had attracted him in her writing were equally present in her person, and he was soon deeply interested in her.

Wells's emotional life was without real focus at this time. He and Jane had long since ceased to be lovers, and his liaison with Amber Reeves had been over for three years. He saw "Elizabeth" (Countess Russell, the author of *Elizabeth and Her German Garden*) with some frequency, it is true, but this affair did not keep him from casual encounters—a good many of them, it would seem. Indeed he was passing through an erratic, unstable phase which bored him and alarmed his wife. For her part Rebecca was fascinated by Wells, despite the disparity in their ages and the unheroic impression that he must have made upon her. (Always small in stature, Wells had grown plump in middle age, and his voice remained high-pitched.)

As a girl whose *jeunesse orageuse* had enabled her to write that powerful study of sexual antagonism, "Indissoluble Matrimony," at eighteen,[6] she found herself in the company of most young men overcome by something like the world-weariness that Pater attributes to the Mona Lisa. Her disdain may be illustrated from an episode that occurred some months later. One day she hurried from Fleet Street with a bundle of Divorce Law Reform Union pamphlets in her arms to attend the wedding of a cousin. The bridegroom, a young man from the War Office, elicited this response from her.

> The sun lay on his fair head like a benediction, and no fretful or angry passion had ever lined that boyish brow: only the gentlest words had shaped that mouth. Personal grace of a high order was accentuated by dainty dressing: his frock-coat fitted him like the pelt of a young antelope, and his trousers had a silvery gleam like willows seen at twilight. He was like a pure white rose.

Confronted by "the Dresden-like charm" of this "decorative person," whose appearance was "such that no one could raise a hand against him save in the way of kindness," Rebecca felt that the obligation to be chivalrous was entirely on her side, so much more experienced was she, so much more aware of life in its darker aspects.[7] Wells, however, was a very different sort of man, renowned in a sense that even Rebecca respected, wise in the ways of the world, and reputed to be dangerous with women.

In the months that followed, Rebecca and Wells saw each other with increasing frequency. His one surviving letter of this period, which dates from early February 1913,[8] implies both an existing intimacy and an impending shift towards an even closer relationship.

Dear Rebecca.

You're a very compelling person. I suppose I shall have to do what you want me to do. But anyhow I mean to help you all I can in your great adventure.

You consider me an entirely generous and sympathetic brother in all your arrangements.

I'll help you all I can and I'll take the risk of its being known about and misunderstood and I trust you implicitly to do your best that it isn't known about.

I post this in London. I've matinéed my small boys today and I motor home this evening (Wednesday).

Tomorrow I get up again about six P.M.

Friday my wife comes home from Switzerland and we go to Little Easton.

H. G.

Meanwhile, Rebecca had left the *Freewoman,* which in any event was about to cease publication, and had resumed a connection with Robert Blatchford's socialist weekly, the *Clarion.* There she had a larger and less specialized audience as well as more space in which to develop her ideas on the women's movement; yet in some ways the change was not propitious. Instead of being able to reflect at leisure on books and experience, she had become a hard-pressed journalist with a tight deadline, charged with bringing current events to the bar of militant feminism. Her *Clarion* articles came to lack the personal, reflective stamp that had marked her work for the *Freewoman* as she was increasingly caught up in the passions of the feminist cause, passions which raged with particular violence at this period because the Women's Suffrage amendment to the Franchise Bill was in the process of being defeated. Exacerbated by the repressive actions of constituted authority, Rebecca gradually threw aside all restraints on her writing. Her revulsion reached its climax in a tirade of 18 April 1913, called "The Sex War," most of the paragraphs in which end with the refrain: "Oh, men are miserably poor stuff."

For Rebecca this refrain had a highly personal application. Though no letters remain from this period, what happened between Wells and her is clear. As they came to know each other better, their conversation, which had previously been kept carefully to books and current events, gradually took a more personal turn. Quite suddenly Rebecca found herself in love. Wells too was profoundly attracted, but he was also doubtful about involving himself with still another young girl, and a few weeks later he broke with her. At the time Rebecca was utterly baffled and humiliated by the cant phrases with which Wells so abruptly turned her

away. In after years she learned that he had sought
to terminate his long-standing relationship with "Elizabeth," only to be impelled by her moving protest
to break with Rebecca instead. Jane strongly sup-
ported this decision, feeling that, since Wells must
have a mistress, one to whom she was accustomed
(and who had, moreover, a visitable chalet in Switzerland) was to be preferred.[9]

The two ensuing months were perhaps the most
crucial of Rebecca's life. Her own account of this
time, a remarkable human document, survives in the
forgotten pages of an obscure magazine. To read it
is to remember that like Yeats, to whose poetry she
was devoted, Rebecca held passionately to the tragic
view of life. If the things that mattered, "like beauty
or love or pride," could be bought only with a
"ritual of rashness and cruelty," [10] she was prepared
to pay the price. When her rage grew too great to be
contained, she would fling herself out of London to
some little somnolent south coast town, there to find
relief in "contemplating the innocent activities of
the natives." The state of mind in which she found
herself after Wells rejected her required a more decisive distraction, and early in May she set off for
Spain accompanied by her mother. On the train,
though she realized the absurdity of her behavior,
she could not keep herself from announcing to her
chance fellow-travelers that "things being as they are
she wanted a vote." They regarded her, she recalled,
"as one might a rebellious chocolate cream." At first,
"ravaged and distorted Spain" with its "naked hills"
and "burning valleys" was so exactly consonant with
her mood as to have a soothing effect. It was only

when she reached Valladolid that her troubles could no longer be borne.

What had happened to Rebecca may be dimly discerned in "At Valladolid," published in the *New Freewoman* of 1 August 1913. It would be misleading to quote this vivid narrative at length, since it is more fiction than autobiography. Yet it is clearly compounded not only of Rebecca's misery at home and the suicide of a girl whom she had known well at the Royal Academy of Dramatic Arts and afterwards, but also of her experience after her rejection by Wells. The narrator through whom Rebecca is speaking relates how she confided in a Valladolid doctor, to whom she had gone for treatment of a bullet wound that had broken open. It is late at night, and the physician, a stolid, heavy man, resents her and the trouble that she is giving him, but she must pour out her confession.

She tells how, "though my lover had left my body chaste he seduced my soul: he mingled himself with me till he was more myself than I am and then left me." Living becomes so painful that "death is an urgent need," but she finds that she is like a black cat that had once survived all her family's attempts to put it away. She takes a massive dose of veronal, but this leads only to a night of drugged wandering about London. Then she shoots herself, aiming at her heart, but missing.

> Those who loved me gathered round me as I lay on the brink of death and dragged me back, tearing my flesh with the sharp teeth of their love. My mother sat by my bed and cried from

the collar-bone, sobs that scald the throat. My
sisters moved reproachfully about the room,
saying to me with their deep-set eyes, "So you
meant to leave us, after we have gone so loyally
with you through all these years of poverty and
tragedy."

She decides that she must go on living. The Spanish
trip on which she embarks is a search for relief from
unbearable pain. It has not come, but she will not
take the way out offered by her wound. So the story
ends, with its narrator's fate left undetermined.[11]

Wells, of course, was the lover who had seduced
Rebecca's soul, as she saw it. In April of the previous
year she had reviewed a performance of *The Seagull*
in the *Freewoman,* and one may surmise that the role
she now conceived herself to be playing bore some
resemblance to that of Nina, the "seagull" of Chekov's play. Nina dies, it will be remembered, after
her desertion by Trigorin, "the successful novelist,
who regards the art rather as a matter of personal
achievement than as the due he must pay to life, and
who is so insensible to the sacredness of emotion that
when a young girl offers him her love he says, as one
would of a medicine, 'Perhaps this is the very thing I
need.' " [12] And Rebecca no doubt expected Wells to
be prominent among the people who would "notice
the gap and be appalled by the violence of its making" if "she cut herself out of life," though she disavows this motive in her narrative. At any rate this
delirious outpouring helped to purge Rebecca of
what was tormenting her, and she continued on her
way through Spain, comforted by both the austerity

and the earthiness of Spanish life. On her return to England at the end of the month she was able to face her world once more.

Meanwhile, Wells was spending May in Italy (his absence was no doubt a factor in Rebecca's flight to Spain), unaware of what had happened to her. When word reached him of the reasons put forward to account for her absence, "bronchitis and injuries" incurred presumably in a suffragist disturbance, he wrote her a chiding letter:

> Why do you engage in these struggles and why do elderly ladies go provoking outrages from policemen? Don't any of you understand that man is a savage animal, imperfectly domesticated, and a large part of the art of living for men and women alike is never to give anyone the ghost of a chance of throwing you downstairs or taking you by the neck. We've got civilization up to the point of really stopping unprovoked assaults, but provoked assaults![13]

Upon his return to London he invited her to "come and talk" at his new flat at 52 St. James's Court.[14] By this time in his life his experience with emotional disturbed young women was sufficiently extensive to have made him wary and skeptical, and he seems to have listened to her story without much sympathy. At any rate, their meeting and the renewed association on terms of casual friendship to which it led caused Rebecca to write the following letter to him. (It may be the original which she decided after all not to send, or it may be a copy which she retained. In either case it is the most considerable document to survive the general holocaust of her letters to him.)

Dear H.G.,

During the next few days I shall either put a bullet through my head or commit something more shattering to myself than death. At any rate I shall be quite a different person. I refuse to be cheated out of my deathbed scene.

I don't understand why you wanted me three months ago and don't want me now. I wish I knew why that were so. It's something I can't understand, something I despise. And the worst of it is that if I despise you I rage because you stand between me and peace. Of course you're quite right. I haven't anything to give you. You have only a passion for excitement and for comfort. You don't want any more excitement and I do not give people comfort. I never nurse them except when they're very ill. I carry this to excess. On reflection I can imagine that the occasion on which my mother found me most helpful to live with was when I helped her out of a burning house.

I always knew that you would hurt me to death some day, but I hoped to choose the time and place. You've always been unconsciously hostile to me and I have tried to conciliate you by hacking away at my love for you, cutting it down to the little thing that was the most you wanted. I am always at a loss when I meet hostility, because I can love and I can do practically nothing else. I was the wrong sort of person for

you to have to do with. You want a world of
people falling over each other like puppies, people to quarrel and play with, people who rage
and ache instead of people who burn. You can't
conceive a person resenting the humiliation of
an emotional failure so much that they twice
tried to kill themselves: that seems silly to you. I
can't conceive of a person who runs about light-
ing bonfires and yet nourishes a dislike of flame:
that seems silly to me.

You've literally ruined me. I'm burned down
to my foundations. I may build myself again or I
may not. You say obsessions are curable. They
are. But people like me swing themselves from
one passion to another, and if they miss smash
down somewhere where there aren't any passions at all but only bare boards and sawdust.
You have done for me utterly. You know it.
That's why you are trying to persuade yourself
that I am a coarse, sprawling, boneless creature,
and so it doesn't matter. When you said, "You've
been talking unwisely, Rebecca," you said it with
a certain brightness: you felt that you had really
caught me at it. I don't think you're right about
this. But I know you will derive immense satisfaction from thinking of me as an unbalanced
young female who flopped about in your draw-
ing-room in an unnecessary heart-attack.

That is a subtle flattery. But I hate you when
you try to cheapen the things I did honestly and
clearly. You did it once before when you wrote
to me of "your—much more precious than you
imagine it to be—self." That suggests that I pro-

jected a weekend at the Brighton Metropole
with Horatio Bottomley. Whereas I had written
to say that I loved you. You did it again on Friday when you said that what I wanted was some
decent fun and that my mind had been, not exactly corrupted, but excited, by people who
talked in an ugly way about things that are really
beautiful. That was a vile thing to say. You once
found my willingness to love you a beautiful and
courageous thing. I still think it was. Your spinsterishness makes you feel that a woman desperately and hopelessly in love with a man is an in-
decent spectacle and a reversal of the natural
order of things. But you should have been too
fine to feel like that.

I would give my whole life to feel your arms
round me again.

I wish you had loved me. I wish you liked me.

Yours,
Rebecca

Don't leave me utterly alone. If I live write to
me now and then. You like me enough for that.
At least I pretend to myself you do.[15]

This appeal also left Wells unmoved. His answer to
Rebecca's letter, or to another in the same vein, was
brief and cool: "How can I be your friend to this accompaniment? I don't see that I can be of any use or
help to you at all. You have my entire sympathy—
but until we can meet on a reasonable basis, good
bye."[16]

CHAPTER III *Rebecca Wooed*

In a postscript to his letter Wells promised to look
for Rebecca's work in the *New Freewoman,* which had
just begun to appear. There she published three articles—"Trees of Gold," "Nana," and the already
mentioned "At Valladolid"—in which she told of her
nightmare Spanish trip with a literary power which
she had not begun to approach in her earlier work.
Wells was shaken out of his attitude of cautious re-
serve by the naked yet controlled passion of these remarkable pages. Henceforth he was in effect to repeat to Rebecca again and again: "I loved your clear
open hard hitting generous mind first of all," [1] refer-
ring, one may surmise, far more to these articles
than to the contributions to the original *Freewoman*
which first· attracted his attention. In any event, he
made the following overture to her in early July.

You are writing gorgeously again. Please resume being friends. You've had time to see just
how entirely impossible it is for you to get that

pure deep draught of excitement and complete
living out of me and how amiable and self deny-
ing it has been of me to refuse to let you waste
your flare-up—one only burns well once—on
my cinders. Nana was tremendous. You are as
wise as God when you write—at times—and
then you are a tortured, untidy . . . little disaster of a girl who can't even manage the most ele-
mentary trick of her sex. You are like a beautiful voice singing out of a darkened room into
which one gropes and finds nothing.

Anyhow I read you with unquenchable
amazement.[2]

But now it was Rebecca who did not respond.
Through writing her Spanish articles she was dis-
covering resources within herself which were to
change her whole outlook on life. She had achieved
a new ability to rise above personal involvements, to
understand not only what was happening to herself,
but also how her experiences were related to the
general experience of mankind. Listening to Nana, a
cafe singer in Seville who held her audience en-
tranced by her opulent body and sympathetic feeling
for their common life, Rebecca had been visited by a
flash of revelation.

I remembered how I once saw the sun beating
on the great marbled loins and furrowed back
of a grey Clydesdale and watched the backward
thrust of its thigh twitch with power. I was then
too interpenetrated with interests of the soul
and the intellect to understand the message of
that happy carcass: if my earliest childhood had

realised that the mere framework of life is so
imperishable and delicious that with all else lost
it is worth living for, I had forgotten it. Now
Nana's dazzling body declared it lucidly: "Here
am I, nothing but flesh and blood. When your
toys of the mind and the spirit are all broken,
come back to my refreshing flesh and blood!" [3]

The broader import of her discoveries is set forth in
"Trees of Gold":

One has to use flame to burn the galoons [gaudy
trimmings] from Europe and the tame squalor
from life, and in the end one may so easily turn
this weapon of fire on oneself. By the heat of its
desires and adorations the mind may become
like hot wax: incapable of receiving the sharp
impressions which are all it lives for. The fire by
whose blaze the soul meant to lighten the world
may burn it down to its foundations and leave it
a smoking ruin, as unlovely as any factory or
building designed from the first for base uses.
The fervent purpose may destroy its instrument
and die frustrated. It brings not only personal
disaster but it is a treachery against the orderly
procession of generation after generation, which
we call life. The poor hurt the community in
which they live: they fall into ugly ways of life,
they spread disease, they leech the stores of the
kind. So too the tragic hurt the community: they
live impulsively, they spread excitement, they
make preposterous demands on the patience
and service of those of good-will. They wreck
the peace for which the race must seek for the
sake of the future. [4]

This new view of her world gradually came to
dominate Rebecca's writing. When she resumed her
contributions to the *Clarion* in mid-June, her first articles were still bitterly political (in describing the fu-
neral of a suffragist leader she even managed to
compare Asquith to Jack the Ripper),[5] but her fierce-
ness soon tapered off. She was increasingly possessed, so she wrote, "by a passion for the peace and
order in which alone wisdom and art can be made," [6]
and mere fidelity to her "sense of humour and sense
of beauty" [7] soon prevented her from following the
suffragist party line. So she allowed herself, writing
as "one completely ignorant young woman to another," to point up the absurdity of a tract called
"The Dangers of Marriage," by Mrs. Pankhurst's
daughter Christabel.[8] If this sacrilege was poorly received by her militant colleagues, they were even
more distressed when she proceeded in her next article to underline the similarities between vengeful
females who hound men for immoral conduct and
southern whites who castrate and lynch Negroes for
raping white women.[9] What compounded Rebecca's
offense in this series of articles was their superior
quality. Her breadth of outlook, her compassion,
and her humor had made her one of the great con-
troversialists of an age of notable literary journalism.
At the very moment when she showed herself to be
women's answer to Shaw, Chesterton, and Wells, she
had lost her faith in the suffragist cause.

It is perhaps the humor of these articles that
marks them off most sharply from her earlier polemical work. Rebecca's eye for the absurd had always
been a potent weapon in her literary armory. In the
Freewoman, for example, she had punctured a pomp-

ous academic survey of contemporary writing with
the following aside:

> I must confess that the passage which gives me
> the most tranquil pleasure is an entry in the
> index:
> "Sex, The unimportance of, p. 224."
> This is Napoleonic. One yearns to grovel, just a
> little.[10]

And her first contributions to the *Clarion* are occasionally lightened by passages such as this:

> For a certain reason I hear the word "womanly"
> with alarm. It recalls a painful incident that oc-
> curred to my sister and me some years ago in a
> public park at Harrogate. We were selling
> "Votes for Women," and we offered one to a
> dear old lady in rustling black silk and widow's
> bonnet. With superb vigour she raised her um-
> brella and brought it down on my sister's head,
> remarking: "Thank God I am a womanly
> woman." [11]

But with her broad new perspective came a com-
mand of the *reductio ad absurdum* which made her articles positively rollicking. So when Belfort Bax
urged in *The Fraud of Feminism* that women should
be grateful because English criminal law deals less
harshly with them than with men, she turned Bax's
illustrations back upon their author with fiendish in-
genuity.

> It makes one wonder. Can it be that we are
> spoiled darlings of our lords and masters, who

have no right to ask for decent pay for our work
because we are so hansomely tipped for our sex?
Why was it that I had never noticed this atmosphere of tenderness and inexhaustible charity?
Could it be because I have not yet stood in the
dock?

That is it. I have never gone away to yacht in
the Mediterranean on money borrowed from a
blind and paralysed husband whom I have left
in Marylebone Union with a stream of solicitors'
clerks depositing on his hard pillow writs of
libels and slanders that I have committed, to say
nothing of my legal claim for maintenance. Nor,
after dragging my husband to bankruptcy by my
reckless enterprises, have I forced him to pay
out his last penny so that I can advertise my
business in the divorce court. I have never per-
jured myself in a breach of promise action. I
have never thrown vitriol over even a private,
and my relations with the local postman are formal but friendly. (How one's
NEGATIVE VIRTUES
mount up!) I could never purloin goods to the
amount of £150 before I was caught, and no
employer would keep me long enough as a clerk
to give me time to get more than the petty cash.
Indeed my inherent disabilities shut me out
from any participation in this feast of chivalry
and goodwill.[12]

Wells responded to Rebecca's strength as he never
had to her abnegation. He told her that her severe
review of his novel *The Passionate Friends* was "first

rate criticism." [13] As she freed herself from her
preoccupation with feminism in the *Clarion,* he
greeted each new article with enthusiasm. "How
much harder one can hit Mr. Asquith through absurdity," he wrote in a typical letter. "Your phrases
about Wright's sentences that ought to have a little
meaning in their arms, are perfect. I shall repeat
them on my death bed. Go on writing. Not on votes
but on doing things superbly well rests all the future
of women." [14] He offered her advice on how best to
further her career, urging her to collect her early articles and reviews into a book called *From the Junior
School,* and the later pieces into another called *Experi-
ments in Experience,* or better still to "lump them all
together and call it *The Taste of Life.*" [15]

Gratified as she was by these advances, Rebecca yet
maintained her independence. In her review of *The
Passionate Friends,* though she preferred it to *Marriage* and praised its many fine passages, she took
issue with Wells's attitude to life: "this perpetual
deprecation of rash defiances, this tolerance of
flinching and weakness, this constant subordination
of the quick personal wisdom to the slow collective
wisdom." Particularly in the novel's style she detected a sharp falling off from *Tono-Bungay* and *The
New Machiavelli.* "It is the pusillanimous effort of a
fierce brain to seek conformity with the common
tameness, the lapse of a disorderly prophet who does
not see that to be orderly is to betray his peculiar
gospel." [16] When Wells asked her to help him edit
and condense certain of his manuscripts for a book
(probably those which eventually went into *Boon*),
she refused.[17] When he urged her to take account of

an article by Chesterton in order to avoid falling into "Webbery," [18] she responded by vigorously attacking the article under the title "Mr. Chesterton in Hysterics." [19]

CHAPTER IV *Panther and Jaguar*

This was the way matters stood when Wells returned to England in November 1913 from another trip to Italy. By this time he had quarrelled with "Elizabeth" and was not only free but eager for another companion. No letters have survived to suggest how he and Rebecca were reconciled, but it is clear that they soon became lovers.[1] At first their relationship was turbulent. In an angry moment, when he feared that Rebecca might leave him, Wells intentionally omitted his usual precautions in the hope that pregnancy might bind her to him. But soon mutual confidence was complete. By early December they were exchanging notes of endearment from "Jaguar" to "Panther." "There is NO Panfer but Panfer," runs one of these, "and she is the Prophet of the most High Jaguar which is Bliss and Perfect Being."[2] Wells added on another occasion: "You are the sweetest of company, the best of friends, the most wonderful of lovers. Thank you for 10,000 things."[3] A little later he wrote: "I've been home two hours

and twice I've turned round to say something to
you—and you weren't there! My dear Panther it's
like the feeling of suddenly missing a limb." [4]

By this time Rebecca had left the family home of
Fairliehope in Hampton Garden Suburb, to which
she did not return, and was living at 28 Clifton Gardens, Maida Vale, with occasional visits to the house
of Mrs. Townshend, an older friend who resided at
36a Langridge Road, Earl's Court. She and Wells
saw each other frequently in London, where he
would sometimes carry her off for a few hours to
rooms at 119 Warwick Street in Pimlico let by a sympathetic Mrs. Strange. Their situation as lovers and
"confederates" necessitated ambiguous telegrams to
Little Easton Rectory and ingenious arrangements
for apparently accidental encounters. So we find
Wells writing:

> At 12 o'c I am coming to Mrs. T[ownshend] for
> a private talk—oh! about nuffing. But if you will
> keep out of the way until about 20 minutes to 7
> and then appear I will take you off. I will say
> are you going eastward—if so come with me. [5]

For a time Rebecca's only confidante was Violet
Hunt, though Letty was eventually admitted to her
secret.

As we have seen, Rebecca was in theory, at least, a
fully emancipated young woman. Again and again in
her early writings she had remarked on "the havoc
men and women make of life if they refuse to love
life for its own sake, but covet the trappings
thereof." [6] She was contemptuous of the "domestic
woman," and she had no faith either in marriage or

in the social system that defended it. Her "great adventure" had always included the possibility of a liaison such as she now entered upon with Wells.

Wells had also been insisting for many years that society's arrangements concerning marriage were hopelessly wrong-headed, but at the same time he had come to entertain a healthy fear of the penalties that society could impose on those who violated its code. He was not far, indeed, from acquiescing in Tartuffe's contention that

> Le scandale du monde est ce qui fait l'offence
> Et ce n'est pas pêcher que pêcher en silence.

Hence, like Benham in *The Research Magnificent,* he had to admit to "a sort of backstairs and under side to his existence." He "needed *bite* in his life," and instead of "smugging about in a state of falsified righteousness," he too allowed himself to "roll in women, . . . rollick in women." [7]

But casual philandering was one thing, and a lasting affair with a young woman of genius was another. Wells's time with Amber Reeves had impressed upon his mind the inconvenience, deceit, jealousy, and inevitable disillusionment that such an attachment held in store for both parties. These memories had no doubt prevailed when he broke with Rebecca earlier in the year. Yet at the same time he was sick of his habit of promiscuousness and of the dubious women with whom it brought him into contact. And so it happened that he overcame his own scruples as well as Rebecca's resistance.

Moreover, Wells was in love as he had never been since his first years with Isabel. His comradeship

with Rebecca was more complete even than that
which he had once enjoyed with Jane. In Rebecca he
at last found a partner whose intellect and imagination, though very different from his own, were not
inferior to them. Not that passion was in any way
subordinated. "It is the most wonderful thing living
clean and simple again," he told Rebecca. "You don't
know the ugly creases you have taken out of my
mind." [8] So it was that Wells at the age of forty-six
found himself committed to a serious affair with a
girl of twenty.

It was understood from the first that theirs was a
union of equals—insofar as equality was feasible between a young, eager girl and an older, experienced
man—that they were to be two writers living, working, and loving together. "Men should never govern
women," Rebecca had written in the *Clarion*, "for it
makes the man purr with self-admiration, and the
woman whine with self-contempt." [9] Patient Griselda
always seemed to her a "sickening beast." [10] Wells
had not tamed Rebecca, he had won her.

Wells also made it plain to Rebecca that she had
no reason to feel guilty with regard to Jane. For
many years it had been agreed that, though the
Wells household would present a respectable front
to the world, he was at liberty to lead his emotional
life elsewhere. Though Jane took no overt notice of
the affair, she was as completely informed about Rebecca as she had been in the past about Amber and
"Elizabeth." One may suspect, indeed, that her chief
initial response was relief at seeing her erratic husband quietly settled in a new pattern.

Perhaps the clearest insight into the nature of the

love between Rebecca and Wells comes from the pet
names by which they called each other: Panther and
Jaguar. They appear to have been the invention of
Rebecca,[11] who in her life with Wells reverted for a
time to the warmth of her childhood circle before
"she had been tripped into the snare of growing
up." [12] She had always been fond of animals, and
when her family moved from rural Scotland to London, she and her sisters made up imaginary replace-
ments for their lost pets. "I should love to be a cat,"
she had written in early April, "and lie in a basket by
the fire all day and go on the tiles at night. And the
life of a tiger seems attractive: even in captivity. It
must be great fun to escape from a menagerie and
liven up a rural district." [13] We have seen how a few
days later at a time of deep trouble she found her
counterpart in a forlorn and ill-omened black cat
that the Fairfields had to turn out of their home.

Panther and Jaguar were far more than mere affectionate nicknames. They stood for the whole attitude towards life evolved by Rebecca and Wells, who
continued to use these names as long as their love
lasted. They emphasized the ruthless withdrawal
from society that the relationship entailed, the fact
that Rebecca and Wells were not part of the pack
and did not acknowledge its law. Instead they were
"carnivores" living apart in their hidden "lair," going
forth to "catch food," and meeting "at the trodden
place in the jungle." [14] Wells's other life at Little
Easton Rectory became a mere "showcase for weekends," from which he escaped to be "loose in London." [15]

The names implied the free recognition by Re-

"Vigil," Panther and Jaguar, added as a frontispiece to *The Great State* (1912), a symposium by Wells and others, which he presented to Rebecca in 1913 with the caution "private and confidential only to be shown to really *safe* people"

becca and Wells of the animal side of their love, their
delight in the sheer physical well-being of a couple in
happy union. On the many occasions when an irre-
sistible impulse to be "loving but obscene" [16] seized
Wells, the cat metaphors to which he resorted at
least saved his letters from mere grossness. He wrote
of Rebecca's "dear fur," of coming up to London for
"a snatch at your ears and a whisk of the tail." [17] Indeed, his way of saying that love would not be possible at a coming meeting was to note that Rebecca was
not "functioning as a Panther." And he confirmed
his abandonment of promiscuity by telling her that
he was "Monogamous not Polygamous Jaguar
now." [18]

Moreover, the names aided Wells in giving his
fancy free rein in his letters to Rebecca. He was wonderfully inventive in playing with feline imagery, not
merely verbally but in scores of little drawings, showing Rebecca and himself as cats, sometimes as panther and jaguar, but more often as smaller domestic
creatures. Even among the surviving "Hundred Up"
scores, which show the players elated or downcast according to the fortunes of the game, there are a few
which show Rebecca and himself in this guise.

Though none of Rebecca's letters remain from
this period, her state of mind can be seen in her
three final articles for the *Clarion*. Her withdrawal
from this polemical journal was entirely her own
doing, Blatchford being always her admiring and
sympathetic supporter, but its logic is abundantly
shown in these high-spirited contributions. "Much
Worse than Gaby Deslys" finds her defending this
"magnificent straight-backed chorus girl," who had

Wells defeated at "Hundred Up"

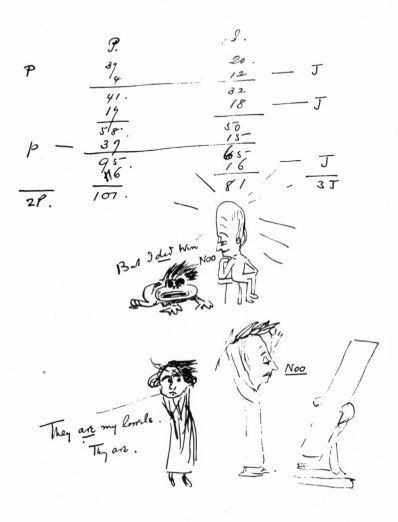

Wells victorious at "Hundred Up"

matured by Rebecca's calculations into a ripe forty-
five, against the Bishop of Kensington's scandalized
criticism of the brevity of her costume. Mlle Deslys,
Rebecca urged, was one of the

> really wonderful and praiseworthy achievements
> of humanity. . . . When she crossed the Palace
> stage she turned the audience's thoughts to May
> mornings, and ices, and money enough to go
> where you like. Now if most of us crossed the
> Palace stage, we would turn the audience's
> thoughts to November evenings, and cold cocoa
> and thirty shillings a week in the Post-office with
> the prospect of threepence a month extra under
> the Holt Report. . . . All that we know of mo-
> rality is that it must be the kind of conduct that
> is instinctive to a healthy body. . . . A healthy
> body means a strong, sensitive nervous system
> that will perceive and understand the emotions
> of others, thereby ensuring an unpriggish altru-
> ism which is the secret of virtue. Therefore I
> believe that the sight of beautiful persons is a
> moral tonic.[19]

It was this article that caused Wells to write to her:
"You dear clear-headed thing. You straight *clean*
thing. You darling. You best of gifts. I have been
reading this week's Clarion." [20]
　　Still more significant as an index to Rebecca's outlook is "Some Race Prejudices" of the following
week. Here she tells how politics have come to seem
to her "a monster that we English have brought
forth to our own destruction," and how "purged of
political passion" she found herself able at last to

"enjoy London unregenerated." The lesson in this experience, she argued, was to "distrust the pack system," the tendency of human beings to herd together because they are miners, or bricklayers, or, presumably, suffragists. There are really only two packs, "the aimless animals that paw the dust obediently, and Hounds of Heaven that urge them on to achievements of the intelligence." [21] Her final article, "The Sin of Self Sacrifice," was an admission that her occupation on the *Clarion* was gone. Henceforth she would speak, not for any party, but for herself. "There is nothing behind the race but the individuals. . . . The people who draw down salvation on life are the people who insist on self-realisation whether it leads to death or gaiety." [22]

CHAPTER V *Hunstanton*

The approach of Christmas, 1913, was a signal for Wells to return to Little Easton Rectory. He and Rebecca were separated for a fortnight, most of which she spent with Violet Hunt at Knap Cottage in Selsey. When she fell ill, Wells's reaction was characteristically free from cant: "You *must* get well because sickness and illness take the Magic out of life. Sick Panthers become little Rebeccas and Jaguars become kind and attentive Fathers and there can be no more love making until the creature is bounding well again." [1] By early January Rebecca was installed in a nursing home in Bulstrode Street. In announcing an approaching visit some days later, Wells found it prudent to assure her that he was "a moral pure quiet Jaguar, suitable for nursing and a position of trust, all the Lamentable Coarseness has gonè out of him." [2]

Meanwhile, it was discovered that Rebecca was pregnant. She moved to the country branch of her London nursing home, the Wood Cottage, Shere

Jaguar lying in wait for Rebecca, 1914

Lane, Chorley Wood, where Wells visited her, vary-
ing walks to Chesham in fine weather with excursions to London when it rained, while he cast about
for a permanent country haven. "Llandudno would
work wonderfully," he wrote in mid-January. "I
could have all my household camped in Bourne-
mouth, or along that coast and lead a double life
with the utmost ease." [3] This unlikely location seems
to have been suggested by Wells's solicitor, E. S. P.
Haynes, then their chief confidant.

Before the removal could be effected, however,
Wells set off on a three-week trip to Russia. The
series of love letters that ensued are equally divided
between Wells's demonstrations of his tender yet
passionate absorption in Rebecca and a graphic and
amusing chronicle of his experiences. Passing
through Berlin, he assured her that he was immune
to the temptations of that sinful city. "I go through
this horde of sensual beasts like a Tennysonian
knight. I exercise no self control, but I just can't
think of any delyts but Panther's delyts." [4] Arriving
in Russia he wrote that "St. Petersburg is more like
Rebecca than any capital I have seen, alive and dark
and untidy (but trying to be better) and mysteriously
beautiful." [5] "Get Wales ready," he told her in his
next letter. "I think of that happy thing cuddled up
in your soft flesh and your dear warm blood. I'm so
glad we've made it." [6] His plans for the household
that he and Rebecca were to establish read like the
scenario for a novel:

You are M[rs] West, I am M[r] West. Write and arrange that you are to stay at Llandudno until

your baby is born. M⸗ West is in the cinemato-
graph business, and he has to write things. He
wants a quiet room to work in and he has to
have a separate bedroom. (Though he proposes
to spend much time in your delicious bed.) You
also write. Make this clear and get everything
comfortably arranged. That house has to be our
home. We have to settle down and work there
and love there and live there, and you have to
see that it is all right. You have got to take care
of me and have me fed and have me peaceful
and comfortable. You are going to be my wife.
We will have great mysteries in each other's
arms, we shall walk together and eat together
and talk together. You are the woman and you
are to be the maker and ruler in all this life. Our
income is about £400 or £450 a year. Panther I
love you as I have never loved anyone. I love
you like a first love. I give myself to you. I am
glad beyond any gladness that we are to have a
child. I kiss your feet. I kiss your shoulders, and
the soft side of your body. I want to come into
the home you are to make for me, I shall hurry
home for it. Get it ready. Make it our success. I
will go down with you there after the 20th. Come
up to London for some days and get clothes and
things to be the young wife of a decent intelligent man.[7]

Rebecca was by this time in correspondence with a
Llandudno landlady. Along with anxious directions
regarding the line to take in these negotiations,

Wells offered advice concerning her general pattern of behavior:

> Don't give anyone your address. Keep up a legend that you are going to live with the Townshends, use that as your address and make vague promises to people to see them and go out with them to things in May and June. It will leave us far freer with each other and it will save Jane enormous embarrassment *if our secret is kept*.[8]

He also sought to prepare her for the inevitable periods of separation that his double life would necessitate once she was remote from London. Even the first few days after his return could not be entirely hers. He would have to spend the weekend at Little Easton Rectory, if only to tell the "Dunmow people . . . that I am wild with a great idea for a book and must go off alone to write it."[9] His awareness of the need for secrecy was no doubt enhanced by his discovery that in Russia at least he was an authentic celebrity who attracted crowds of admirers wherever he went. "Jaguars do not know how to behave in such circumstances. They are scared by a sense of unavoidable visibility. I want to get behind the jungle reeds at Llandudno and write."[10]

Wells's reunion with Rebecca took place in mid-February. After putting in an appearance at Little Easton Rectory, he hastened to London where she was waiting for him at Mrs. Townshend's. Two days of love followed at Mrs. Strange's Warwick Street rooms, during which they decided to settle, not at

Llandudno after all, but at Hunstanton on the Norfolk coast, a town which he could reach by train
from Bishop's Stortford without an intervening trip
to London. The ensuing days of preparation saw
Wells "prowling" to Hunstanton to "make a lair
there," advising Rebecca on a sensible wardrobe (a
tweed skirt and jacket and brown boots and good
blow-about head things") [11] and deploring Haynes's
gossip about them:

> I told you all this sort of thing excites Haynes
> beyond sanity. The evenings at St. John's Wood
> are not spent in praising me. But we must go on
> exactly as if the Haynes were our loyal and gen-
> erous friends and such is human nature they
> will presently forget their emotions and become
> so. [12]

About 21 February the long-anticipated move occurred. The trip to Hunstanton was not made without elaborate precautions against discovery, Wells
during its planning describing himself as "an agi-
tated Bradshaw." [13] Despite Rebecca's uncertain
health, they were to travel on different trains from
London, since Wells deemed it too risky to accompany her even in separate carriages. Having met at
Hunstanton station, "Mr. and Mrs. West" went to
Brig-y-don, lodgings kept by a Mrs. Crown on Victoria Avenue. After a week together Wells returned to
London, where by the first of March he was writing
reassuring notes to "dear little sweet Lovely Panther," urging her to "get some work done, good
work, and believe in your Jaguar with all your
heart." [14]

Rebecca and Wells, added as a tailpiece to *The Great State* at Hunstanton in 1914

At Hunstanton, which was to be their home for
half a year, they lived in

> a rawboned house which stood on a cliff facing
> the Wash and casting a sidewise glance to the
> North Sea across bents misted with sea-lavender.
> A lighthouse stood sentinel beside it, and there
> were little white coastguard cottages with cobble-
> stones and a bleaching-green, and near at hand
> a wireless station lifted its gaunt arms. It was
> one of those wholly tedious East Coast districts
> which hold one simply by a wine-like strength in
> the air.[15]

During the months that followed, Wells spent all
the time that he could with Rebecca, occasionally a
week or ten days at a stretch, but usually two or
three days in the middle of the week. His only prolonged absence came in late May and early June,
when after a week's visit to Ireland he was im-
mobilized for ten days at Little Easton Rectory by a
hockey accident to his knee. Rebecca was inevitably
much alone, though Letty and Mrs. Townshend
came to see her, as did Wilma Meikle, a close friend
from her suffragist days. Indeed, she visited the city
not at all during her time at Hunstanton, and when
Wells was informed, by a paragraph in a gossip column or a spoken report, that someone had seen her
there, he wrote ironically: "I'm so glad you're being
seen about London. Clever Panther." [16]
When they were together at Hunstanton, they saw
no company ("The Wests never have entertained,"
Wells was later to remark),[17] but they were happy by
themselves, walking in the woods and along the

shore, driving in a hired car to nearby points of interest, and bathing and boating when warmer
weather came. Wells wrote to a friend at this time:

> If life presses too hard and you want a complete
> change for a day or two, come down and see the
> Wests at Hunstanton (c/o Mrs. Crown Victoria
> Avenue). They have a spare bedroom and are
> kind gossiping creatures. Mrs. West is brown
> and now dreadfully big with young, she has a
> dear ugliness that grows upon the affections.
> Mr. West adores her. They go down on to the
> beach where they have a hut and he bathes and
> then one sits about in a dry bathing suit gossip-
> ing. That is all.[18]

A good part of each day was given to work, Wells oc-
cupying himself with *The Research Magnificent,* and
Rebecca reviewing fiction for the *Daily News.*[19] Wells
deplored these efforts, telling Rebecca that her
"bones *soften* with these novels . . . it isn't good for
the cub." [20] He thought better of the admiring study
of Henry James to which she was devoting herself,
even though he himself had in his portfolio the on-
slaught on James which he was to publish next year
in *Boon.*

When Wells was away, he wrote to Rebecca daily.
His chief aim was to tell her how profoundly he
needed her and how much he loved her. Some of
Wells's notes are in the "wicked" vein, mildly rebuked by Rebecca, that led him to remark: "I don't
imagine any one will ever print my love letters unless
the printer lays in a special fount for lines of
stars." [21] Others emphasize the tender com-

panionship that was the other side of their love.
Here is one of the latter, written in an idiosyncratic
free verse to which Wells had frequent recourse.

Dear little Mate.

Fing I like talking to
Fing I like to sit about with *not* talking
    Person that it's pleasant to be against
    Dear, dusky, dear-eyed Panther
        Warm kind Companion
    The world bores me to death
        (Or rather *my* world does)
    It bores me and irritates me
    When I am away from you.
        I like the feel of you.
        I like the noises you make
        I love your faults
        I love your voice.
        I love your truth
        I love your affectations
            I love you.[22]

Meanwhile, the game of two against the world that
they were playing still held its fascination. "I'm going
to London today to battle with publishers and riff-
raff," runs a representative letter. "Soon as I've got a
kill I shall return to the lair and my happiness." [23]
Yet despite the excitement that continued to attend
their successful dissembling, despite Wells's assurances to Rebecca that "Hunstanton and you are better for me than all the Flesh Pots of Easton," [24] the
inconveniences and irritations of their lodging-house
life had begun to oppress them, and they made

plans for a house of their own into which they could move after the baby's birth, a proper "home" where "idiotic concealment" would be unnecessary.[25]

Their calm routine was shattered by the guns of August 1914. Rebecca's anxiety mounted as the dislocations of war imposed themselves. She sent a telegram to Little Easton Rectory addressed in her agitation to "West." Wells replied with reassurances about money ("Keep your gold and cash for your tradespeople until they are reconciled to notes and pay Mrs. Crown in notes") and provisions ("There's plenty in the country"). He joked about her approaching ordeal:

Don't you go off as a War Correspondent nohow
The First War Correspondent With Child
"What the world is like
An Impression of a Battlefield
By a New Comer."
You prepare your Citizen for the Age of Peace.

There was no need to send for Letty. "I shall come to Hunstanton in my car I expect, if the railway is disordered, so sister need not anticipate Anthony's coming." Wells himself was in high spirits. He found "something bracing . . . in this crisis," and his articles interpreting the war were in great demand both in London and New York.[26]

Rebecca's misgivings turned out to have been amply justified. Anthony Panther West was born on 4 August, the date of England's declaration of war on Germany. She reflected afterwards that by this chance she had lost not only the foreboding of extreme peril, but also the delicious sense of importance which is the consolation of her sex on these occasions. This was motherhood with a difference. When the mists of chloroform cleared away and they held out her squealing son, she looked at him, not with the passive contentment of the mother in peace-time, but with the active and passionate intention: "I must keep this thing safe." [27]

Wells hurried from London to Hunstanton after wiring Jane, who replied:

I am full of misery at your telegram. It isn't Rebecca herself is it who is in danger. I try to think the message might mean the child—not her. Will you wire to me if there is any better news to send? This is horrible. Give her my dear love if you can.[28]

But all turned out satisfactorily, and the following day Wells wrote from Little Easton Rectory to Rebecca, who was attended by Letty and Mrs. Townshend:

I am radiant this morning. With difficulty I refrain from giving people large tips. I am so delighted I have a manchild in the world—of yours. I will get the world tidy for him. . . . I keep on thinking of your dear dear, dear grave sweet belovéd face on your pillow and you and it. I do most tremendous love you Panther.[29]

The days passed with Wells absorbed in his war articles (among them "The War that Will End War"

A jaguar cub and his world, 1914

of 14 August and an appeal to the American people written at the suggestion of Lloyd George), visiting Rebecca every two or three days, and writing to her regularly in the intervals. "I get up and whistle while I write about national catastrophes because I love you," he told her in one of these letters.[30] "I hear you are getting on with that sweet little thing that is going to be a *Great Man*," he wrote in another. "Lie and purr with it and I will manage the world part for a bit." [31] "Nothing to say very much but war, war, war," runs a third. "I kiss my little son's soft hand and the corner of your sweet mouf and I am your very Loving Jaguar." [32]

Wells derived a certain amount of comic relief in these hectic times from Violet Hunt and Ford Madox Hueffer, who were visiting Little Easton Rectory. A month earlier Violet had assured Wells that Rebecca was "just at the fatal age for phthisis. She mourns you already as one dead." [33] Rebecca was indeed subject to serious recurring illness, but in this instance Violet Hunt was ludicrously wide of the

Panther's Column for Young Mothers

How to remove darkstains from our little Darlings.

If Baby falls in the Ink

How I made a Crumb Cloth.

A Pleasant Dish for Irritable Husbands

Fancy Work.   What to do out of Pen Nibs

"Panther's Column for Young Mothers"

mark, and Wells consequently wrote to Rebecca, "V.
H. hasn't an idea of your baby. She said, 'Poor little
girl she can't last long. She's there with a nurse and
people. Phthisis.' " [34]

> Hueffers still abundantly here [Wells continued
> in his next letter]. Much light on the Question of
> the War—Hueffer described how the Emperor
> William talked to him for two hours on the dif-
> ficulties of the German position. Also Hueffer's
> reasons for volunteering for garrison artillery
> were novel and subtle. V. H. neither obtrudes
> nor avoids the West topic. She said incidentally
> you were the sweetest person one could have
> about a house (I knew that). Also she sat with
> that work of hers and talked with a pensive ex-
> perience of how a man can give a woman satis-
> faction.[35]

Somewhat less cheering presumably was the visit
paid to Rebecca by her mother, who had remained
unreconciled to her liaison with Wells. "I hope she
didn't worry you too much," he wrote after Mrs.
Fairfield's departure.[36]

On 18 August Mrs. Townshend sent Wells a letter
about Rebecca which he passed along to her with the
marginal comment: "All this is nonsense, but what a
dear she is." Yet the appraisal it contains is in fact
very shrewd.

> It was delightful to see R.W. with her boy. It
> would be a thousand pities to separate them.
> Suckling is a wonderful calmant.
> Do you see now what a blunder you made

when you said that what she needed was a "young man's life"? You might have known, since its your trade to understand people, that she isn't the kind that keeps sex in a water-tight compartment. She's not a bachelor-woman but all that there is of the most feminine.

A lover at discreet intervals isn't enough for her: she needs a baby and a home as well. Even as a writer she'll do better work if she has them. I don't know how you're going to manage it. I suppose it will have to be one of those alms-houses we talked about but don't have a row of them, even though, as you boast, you are still a first-rate sire and though the nation will need sons. I don't think R. is really suited for polygamy though I admit she would like a 5th of you better than the whole of anyone else.

If I can be of any use, please tell me. I would come up to town at once if there were anything I could do. I would, for instance, look for a cottage or a nurse if you decide on that.[37]

Mrs. Townshend was duly commissioned to look for the "ideal cottage" not too far from Little Easton Rectory, and she finally found it in a house called Quinbury at Braughing, Hertfordshire. Though Braughing was only six miles from Bishop's Stortford and a dozen miles from Dunmow, it seemed safe since it was "quite out of the Stortford world." This time Wells sketched a somewhat different *donnée* to Rebecca for the little drama that they were to play out: "You will take the house as Mrs. Rebecca West whose husband does newspaper work and comes and goes. The nurse and housekeeper had better think it's all right.' . . . It seems almost too good to be true that we shall walk and talk in our own garden, eat at our own table, entertain visitors in our own house." [38]

CHAPTER VI *Braughing and Alderton*

Rebecca was installed at Braughing as Mrs. West before 24 September. In this village farmhouse, situated "among elms on a Roman road and looking itself ancient and living like the trees," she "could stand at her porch under the white creeper and finger the rough sun-crumbled brick and look down the valley of green water-meadows and cherish once more the illusion of stability." The war seemed remote at first, "except for the high price of food and the difficulty of getting coal." Now that she was mistress of her own home, however, the grave difficulties of her irregular position forced themselves upon Rebecca's attention. Though she was only twenty-one, her varied past experience had equipped her to run a normal household with ease, but she soon discovered that finding reputable and competent servants for a sub rosa establishment was a very different matter. Anthony was well looked after by his Irish midwife whose fondness for him had kept her with the family, and there was an amia-

ble maid called Nancy. But as housekeeper Rebecca
had to put up with a gloomy malcontent named Mrs.
Morse. Moreover, wartime life brought its own haz-
ards. There was a cook, for example, who came into
the dining room one night and "began to pour out
obscene tales about the nurse and the housemaid in
the blotted speech of undecided consonants that
comes to the mad." Rebecca discovered that "she had
lost her sweetheart and her three brothers in the
war." At one Point Rebecca had eleven Hampshire
soldiers billeted upon her for several days, but this
turn of events she regarded as a challenge, and she
met it with enjoyment.[1] Wells in his character of Mr.
West was sometimes impatient and irritable at the
resulting domestic discomfort. In the wake of one
small crisis he wrote:

> I'm very sorry if my rotting of you has weak-
> ened your hand. I do dearly love my Panther
> and I will try in future to strengthen rather than
> weaken you. The Visitor business must be got
> straight. I want to be free to come when I like
> and the Visitor's Room to be free only when I
> have clearly arranged for it. A lot of shady visi-
> tors will be bad for the servants and disturbing
> for you. I'll just plant myself in someday and
> stick—no doubt to the astonishment of the visi-
> tors.[2]

As this letter suggests, his own visits from Little
Easton Rectory were more and more frequent, at
first by bicycle but latterly in a new car, soon chris-
tened Gladys, which turned out to be a great success.
    Rebecca by this time was gradually resuming her

normal life. In September Walter Lippmann had proposed that she become a contributor to the *New Republic,* which he was in the process of founding. The arrangement was duly made, despite her initial lack of enthusiasm, and the first of her articles appeared on 7 November. While they were still at Hunstanton, Wells had urged Rebecca to "get a *very* good business-like blue serge suit and a not too aggressive black sort of hat so as to look very square and rational," and in this costume to "come to London as the resolute free woman." [3] She now began to pay occasional visits to the city, whereupon Wells paradoxically complained of her absences from Braughing.

Meanwhile, Wells's virtual abandonment of Little Easton Rectory had led to unhappiness there. Before the outbreak of the war, he and Jane had decided to rebuild this old house into a much more commodious and comfortable residence. As usual, the actual execution of their plans fell on Jane, who managed well enough until work came to an inevitable standstill in August. Then, as the weeks passed, Wells found the turmoil intolerable, and gradually came to divide his time almost entirely between his London flat and Braughing.[4] There were complaints from Jane, but Wells did not alter his routine.[5]

The winter of 1914/15 passed without any essential modification in the pattern that has been sketched. Rebecca was busy with her *Daily News* and *New Republic* articles and her study of Henry James. As the rebuilding of Little Easton Rectory approached completion, Wells once again made it his part-time residence. It was his renewed familiarity

Rebecca's review of Ford Madox Ford's *The Good Soldier* in the *Daily News*, 2 April 1915

with the daily routine there, indeed, that drew him into the writing of *Mr. Britling Sees It Through.* Meanwhile, "Gladys" proved an invaluable resource for country tours with Rebecca.

Yet Braughing was a compromise at best, and Wells found it necessary to write a series of encouraging notes such as the following to reconcile Rebecca to continuing there: "Don't, dear Heart, think life is a failure on the strength of two bad colds and a little discomfort. You are the mate of everything that is peculiarly me, and if we both died of accidental discomfort tomorrow nothing could alter that. Quinbury was and will be again the dearest lair." [6] Servants remained the chief cause of their uneasiness. This problem found dramatic embodiment in an episode which led to the departure of the surly and incompetent Mrs. Morse. Wells had locked £100 in notes and a few sovereigns in a drawer as a resource against wartime emergencies. Rebecca discovered that the drawer had been tampered with and re-

moved the money to another hiding place. Whereupon Mrs. Morse confronted Rebecca in Wells's absence and declared that unless the little hoard were
given to her she would tell Jane of Wells's double
life. Unmoved by this threat, a sufficiently empty
one given the actual situation, Rebecca stood her
ground and Mrs. Morse departed. But she did not
omit to denounce Rebecca at Braughing Rectory,
and once in London she went to Whitehall Court to
expose Wells to Jane. When Wells was shown the letter Mrs. Morse had left, Jane being absent, he was
concerned enough to involve Haynes in coping with
her.[7] For Rebecca, lonely and isolated as she was at
Braughing, the experience was far more serious.
Here were the hostile forces of convention and pro-
priety materializing in her own home in a particularly loathsome, if somewhat farcical, way. Her whole
attitude towards her life with Wells was altered.

By spring there could be no doubt that a radical
change in their arrangements was required. In answer to one of Rebecca's appeals, Wells wrote:

> You know it's as clear as daylight to me that you
> are my love. Mentally, temperamentally, physi-
> cally, I've never been so warm and close with
> anyone as with you. And we have been ragging
> it all to pieces and spoiling it with detailed
> bothers for which we are both indisposed and
> naturally not very capable. . . . Let us for the
> rest of the time regard Quinbury as the joke it
> is—a joke a little against us but still a very amus-
> ing joke, and with much very beautiful too.[8]

They considered various alternatives. To Rebecca's
suggestion that she live with Violet Hunt, who could

certainly claim a good deal of domestic experience, Wells replied:

> Do you think you could endure V.H.'s questions *constantly?* Also how can she let South Lodge with all that bric-a-brac and art nouveau rubbish in it? Go on in the course Heaven has marked out for you and do not worry too much over things of the kitchen.[9]

It was decided finally that Rebecca should move to the vicinity of London. Meanwhile, shortages had led to a general watering of milk in Hertfordshire, and Anthony, a "lusty child, who had been one of those babies of flushed, abundant flesh, became suddenly froglike and unfriendly, waving hostile, helpless hands and wailing a gathering distress." Rebecca, still as Mrs. West, took Anthony for June and July to Maidenhead, "one of those vulgar Thames-side towns, an idiot's paradise of geraniumed houseboats and polished punts." She found life at the Grosvenor House there profoundly depressing. This "Thames-side hotel, which always was a place of grimed plush hangings and gilt cornices, accepted the scarcity of servants as an excuse for a franker filth; and on the lawns by the river degraded old men and French and Belgian *embusqués* got drunk because there was a war." She "longed for the clean order of some country home where summer was not a blowsy female in a motor-launch, but a profitable heat running along the earth to warm it for harvest." [10]

During this period Wells began preparations for Rebecca's change of residence with the following newspaper advertisement:

Family of two with nurse and child (ten months)
want apartments (4 or 5 rooms) in any good
outer suburb, north or west London. Use of garden. Accommodation for small car desirable.
From 3 to 5 guineas a week according to conve-
niences. Permanency. Apply office of the
paper.[11]

But soon afterward he met William Foss, an adven-
turer on the fringe of the theatrical world, who had
a house on Royston Park Road, Hatch End, Pinner,
near Rebecca's friends at Chorley Wood and a half
hour's train ride to central London. She remembers
it as "one of a large colony of Edwardian villas with
large gardens, with no shops for two miles, and no
public transport, which was hardly ideal for wartime." There was some thought at first of sharing the
house with the Fosses, but Foss proved un-
trustworthy and they had to be asked to go. Their
things were packed in a room, and Rebecca was dis-
patched to buy new furnishings, but the house was
too big to be properly equipped from scratch. Still,
by the end of July Rebecca was established after
a fashion at Alderton, now as "Miss West" with
Anthony as her infant nephew and her friend Wilma
Meikle as housekeeper-companion. (The idea of a
"widow West" was proposed but dismissed.)[12] The
household was completed by Miss Morison, an admirable Scottish nurse who went by the name of
Nanky, and two general servants. A visitor's room
was provided for Wells in his new role of friend of
the family. In this villa, which "looked as though yes-
terday its parts had lain unrelated in a builder's

"Pages from the Life of a Victim," 1915

yard," Rebecca lived a "pinched life, . . . saving, pla-
cating servants, trying to do all the plumbing and
carpentering herself." In such a setting the excitement of the zeppelin raids was almost welcome.[13]
Wells's chief aim in thus giving Rebecca her own
home was to overcome her too great reliance on
him. "You ought to write a straight letter as one man
to another to your mother," he had advised her in
June, "pointing out that your one chance of social
rehabilitation and becoming independent of me is
for your family to help your independent home at
Alderton to be a success. Represent me as a peni-
tent." [14]

Under these circumstances Rebecca and Wells did
in fact see a good deal less of each other, though she
sometimes joined him in London for lunch or dinner before the "movies" (to which they were both
devoted), and he was occasionally a midweek guest at
Alderton. They hardly ever went to a play together,
since Wells was afraid that he might be recognized.
Rebecca rebuilt the separate life that Wells desired,
her sisters and friends rallying around. Mrs. Fairfield herself, though she continued to deplore her
daughter's relationship with Wells, welcomed visits
from Rebecca and Anthony.[15] In February of 1916
Rebecca wrote to S. K. Ratcliffe, an English journalist living in the United States who was a friend of the
Fairfield family and had proved helpful in placing
her articles in American magazines:

> Now I am hardly ever allowed to see the Great
> Man, and when I do it is usually in a public hall
> or on some similarly intimate occasion. . . .

I am in the most miserable state. Every thing emotional that has kept me going through the worries and hardships of the last three or four years has suddenly failed me. It is nobody's fault. Devotion and affection are part of my daily life, but my life is simply empty and I am possessed by a terrifying sense that I am growing old and that there are no more peacocks and sunsets in the world. I suppose there always were only a limited number. But how one wants them all! [16]

For a time, indeed, the love of Wells and Rebecca gained a new lease on life from the holiday associations that now attended it. Passion and wit once again predominated over tenderness and sentiment in his letters to her.[17] Even as writers they benefited from this new phase. Wells's dwindling faith in *Mr. Britling* revived after Rebecca praised the manuscript. "It does me no end of good to get you into my work" he told her.[18] And when Rebecca wrote with real enthusiasm of *The Research Magnificent* in the *Daily News,* Wells exclaimed: "A kind review! Panther my heart swelled." [19]

But once more trouble arose with regard to domestic arrangements. Nanky was a treasure, but nothing else was really right. In the spring of 1916 Wells wrote to Rebecca:

I am sorry and perplexed about Alderton. Sooner or later we'll get the perfect menage. Would you like to see Auntie North? She still wants a job. It's a long job I know to get a balanced household. Your "position" isn't all the

Wilma and Rebecca defeated at "Hundred Up"

trouble though of course it aggravates the situation. I think frankly that Wilma is a failure. She does nothing and her presence and manner exasperates the servants. She's companionship—so far as a "hundred up" goes. But she is an unreal discontented person who doesn't know what she is up to. I shall be glad when she is married and off the menu.

The Miss North thus proposed as a companion-housekeeper to replace Wilma Meikle had been a nurse to a neighbor and friend of the Wellses at Easton. Wells went on to describe her:

You know Auntie North is *grey*—a wonderful good cook—an old nurse (chances of a clash with Nanky)—rather quick tempered, touchy, and generous—and able to *manage* any servant. She could probably run the house like a new watch, order and arrange all meals and everything with one able bodied servant. *One* servant has no fellow plotter.[20]

Rebecca did not want anyone from Easton about her home, and she succeeded in fending off Miss North's visit for the time being, but the servant problem remained.

To get away from these annoyances Rebecca in May took lodgings at Bognor with Anthony and Nanky. When she departed after a time for the Riviera Hotel in Maidenhead, her suggestion that Wells join her there elicited an exasperated reply:

I wanted you to go to Monkey Island. I could have come there. The *Riviera* is quite impossible

for me—so I suppose we must now consider
ourselves separated until you get to Hatch End.
It is a bore. But I can't risk our being seen in sin
at that conspicuous place next door to Murrays.
Baerlein's appearance I think settled that con-
clusively. Monkey Island would have been
cheaper, cleaner, safer and I wanted it. I hope
you may presently muddle through to some sort
of possible arrangement. For two years we have
muddled, been uncomfortable and piled up ex-
penditure, your output of work has been trivial,
my work has suffered enormously. . . .
From the Riviera I think you had better come up
to the Savoy, All of which is just cursing.[21]

This flareup was soon extinguished, but Wells's
temper continued to be uncertain, and the summer
of 1916 was punctuated with further tantrums and
apologies.

The great resource of Wells and Rebecca during
this troubled period was Monkey Island. He had
known this tiny and obscure spot in the Thames
near Bray ever since he paid summer visits to his
maternal uncle Tom Pennicott at Surly Hall Inn, half
a mile down river, during his last three years as a
Bromley schoolboy.[22] These were the happiest times
of his youth, and it was natural, since Surly Hall Inn
was no longer in operation, that when Rebecca settled at Alderton, he should have introduced her to
Monkey Island Inn. Rebecca's preference for the Riviera Hotel, mentioned in the letter quoted above,
derived from the fact that she was accompanied by
Anthony and his nurse and did not wish to be

marooned on this virtually inaccessible island in cramped accommodations and without shops. Alone with Wells, however, she was greatly taken with the unspoiled solitude that it offered. It was approached by a poplar-lined private road, one learns from Rebecca's loving description of it in chapter three of *The Return of the Soldier*. From the ferry, marked by a white hawthorn, the visitor looked across to the inn.

> In front were the dark green glassy waters of an unvisited backwater; and beyond them a bright lawn set with many walnut trees and a few great chestnuts, well lit with their candles, and to the left of that a low white house with a green dome rising in its middle and a verandah whose roof of hammered iron had gone verdigris colour with age and the Thames weather. This was the Monkey Island Inn. The third Duke of Marlborough had built it for a "folly," and perching there with nothing but a line of walnut trees and a fringe of lawn between it and the fast full shining Thames it had a grace and silliness that belonged to the eighteenth century.[23]

Here at least Rebecca and Wells could be alone and at peace.

During August and early September Wells made the futile and frustrating tour of the French and Italian fronts described in his *War and the Future: Italy, France and Britain at War*. While he was away, he wrote constantly to Rebecca vacationing at Whitby, absence as usual having the effect of intensifying his love for her. He emphasized his chastity in the face of Parisian temptations, he pretended jealousy of the handsome young men Rebecca was seeing (particularly Hugh Hart, a harmless friend of Rebecca's youth), and he harped constantly on "Monkey Island delights." But he also brooded over the irritations of Alderton, erupting finally into the following protest:

> I wish we could fix up some sort of life that would detach us lovers a little more from the nursery. Of course you can't hide from the eyes of any nurse that you are the child's mother. I want to make love to you and be with you as a lover day and night and to have that all more of a lark and companionship than it is. Wilma. D.P. creaking doors,—it isn't much fun that way. (It's really a very severe test of my love for you.) Can't you fix up some sort of living with your sisters (and Anthony) with me not about, and me and you have a love life together. Go abroad presently and things like that. You think it over. I'm all at your disposal and any scheme that seems hopeful to you I'll back up. I don't at all mind dropping *Alderton*. I wish your mother wasn't so hopelessly hostile. You think out some scheme—you think out any scheme. You see in the nature of things we haven't much more than ten or twelve years more of love and nakedness and all those dear things. It's a pity to so arrange life that we get nothing better than snatched moments of the night together and evenings with those two appalling bores Wilma and Googoo.[24]

A long weekend with Rebecca on Monkey Island after his return failed to pacify Wells. "Clear Wilma out," he told Rebecca. "This is an ultimatum." [25] A few days later he added: "Go on getting rid of Wilma. . . . She *must* go." [26] He offered in return to stay away from Alderton if Rebecca's family would join her there. They would meet instead in a London "love room," preferably a Chelsea studio flat. One of Rebecca's few surviving letters to Wells comes precisely at this juncture:

Dearest Jaguars.

I ates being separated from my Jaguar. Do you realise you were away from me for a month and that I have only seen you twice since? I hate it. I am going up on Monday to see about that studio. There is no life for us separately. Just a few nice hours over our books and articles and then when we can't write any longer an empty feeling.

Your loving Panther.

Wells's reply, jotted on the margin of Rebecca's letter, reads in part:

Me too. Get your little home in order—make it a work place—very *fishient*—get rid of Wilma and all Bores—get your sister and your old circle there—and prepare for thorough lickings in the London studio.[27]

Within the next two days Wells had made "a sort of Warwick Street arrangement *pro tem* at 51 Claverton

Street," where they would be "the married couple
who can't meet somehow at home." [28] As it turned
out, the Chelsea studio was never found; and for the
next two or three years these Claverton Street rooms,
which remained scantily furnished since they were
supposed to be temporary, were their chief London
retreat.

CHAPTER VII *Deep Questioning*

In early March 1917 Rebecca, now fixed in her role of Miss West, moved from Alderton to Southcliffe, Marine Parade, at Leigh-on-Sea in Essex, a charming little house, with a splendid view of the Thames estuary. Despite the longer train journey that resulted, the pattern of Wells's life with her was for a time hardly affected by this change of residence. As before they continued to meet in London at Claverton Street and elsewhere, and Wells paid many midweek visits to her new home.

Servants were still a bother, and when Rebecca's faithful maid Nancy went off to be married she was left with only Nanky, who was eager for an overdue holiday. Rebecca finally gave in to Wells's urging that she take Miss North from Easton as Nanky's temporary replacement. Rebecca found her to be "the worst type of old upper servant, oily, cunning, and mischief-making." Moreover, as it turned out, Miss North regarded herself as a guest rather than a housekeeper. Since she did no work, sitting instead

in the living room where she drank innumerable
cups of tea, she was useless as Nanky's replacement.
Miss North's departure after five days was a profound relief to the entire household. Rebecca was
particularly offended to discover that, on being
asked by Wells to come to Leigh, Miss North had
first sought Jane's approval, and that Wells regarded
it as beautiful in Jane to have told her that she could
come.

Wells did his best to compensate for these and
other annoyances. He spent as much time as he
could manage with Rebecca and Anthony, and when
he was away he sent her letters dotted with little tributes, one of which runs: "Dear Panther. Amoosing
Panther. Panther 1. (won easily) Cleopatra 2. Aspasia
3. The rest nowhere." [1] His success with *God the In-
visible King,* the first book of his brief religious phase,
led to a longer outburst in free verse.

I am a Male
I am a Male
I am a MALE.
I have got Great Britain Pregnant
        She is greater than ever.
    She is full of Theological Discussion
Blessed is Great Britain above all Nations
            Because
        She is full of God.
Theological books are selling
        Selling like Hot Cakes
    And the breasts of my Mother Land
        are tight with the Milk of the Word
As for me I lunch with Liberal Churchmen
    I dine with Bishops.

Lambeth Palace is my Washpot.
Over Fulham have I cast my breeches.
Because I am a Male.
Because I learnt from Panther, how to do these
   things.[2]

The summer brought more formidable trials.
Wells was in poor health, and for a time he and
Rebecca ceased to be lovers. Since the German air-
plane raids, which had begun the previous November, usually followed the Thames estuary, Leigh became a prime target. Rebecca and Anthony narrowly
missed being caught in a Sunday morning bomb attack at nearby Southend, and a few days later she
found her cat dead of machine-gun bullets in the
street outside her house. She had perforce to send
Anthony away just after his third birthday to a
school kept by a friend in London, it being hopefully
assumed that the German planes would not reach
the metropolis. Then, later in the summer, night
raids began, with their attendant sleeplessness and
terror. Already worried and distraught, Rebecca
now realized that London too was unsafe. Her over-
whelming anxiety for Anthony was part of the background to her first open quarrel with Wells, which is
described in a letter he wrote to her in mid-September:

The raid night gave me a shock. My instinct is to
alter or avoid disagreeable things if that can be
done and to sit tight and jeer if it can't. You
behaved like a different sort of animal altogether. I *hated* your going out in the passage
and talking to whoever chanced to be there and
going to the door. The next night when I was

tired and jaded and trying to get away from it
by playing a mechanical patience you set up
loud and exasperating cries of "Oh *God* oh *God!*"
For which I detested you. These trivialities seem
to have released my mind to look at a whole
group of facts that I have refused to look at
before. I thought, "I'm just going on with this
business. Do I love this woman at all?" I
thought, "I've made up a story about her and it
isn't the true one. What is the true one?" As far
as I can make it out it is this. I love your artistic
vigour, your wit, your fat old voice, a real
greatness and beauty that shines through you,
much that you enjoy, and the perfect delight-
fulness of our embraces. Companionship and
desire, that ought to keep two people together.
But there is a shadow which has grown darker
until it blackens out all that. So far as I can make
it out it is this. I am constantly dismissing evil re-
alizations from my mind. The world and everything may be damned but I *won't believe it.* The
whole world may be against me, *the world is
wrong.* That's my temperament, my habit of
mind. You are—otherwise. You go out to get
the fullest impression of any old black thing.
Every disagreeable impression is welcome to
your mind, it grows there. All the past four
years which might have been a love-adventure
in our memories, your peculiar genius has made
into an utterly disagreeable story—which has become the basis for an entire hopelessness about
anything yet to come. A silly woman with a taste
for cinema drama like Mrs. Morse has become

the presiding genius of our lives—she and your mother. Mrs. Morse has destroyed any joint life for us except in those bag littered rooms at Claverton Street. A Dickens character, she was. We never meet but your mother's grizzling because we are not married drops like a corrosive liquid on any happiness there may still be in our meeting. Poor old witch she is to damn two lives like ours. But these people and such people as your nurse, dominate you. I have no power against them. This is not an accusation. I wish it was, because that would mean there was a remedy. If I could wrangle with you and fight for a change there would be some hope in the situation. But this is the statement of an absolute and incurable incompatibility. It is your nature to darken your world and blacken every memory. So long as I love you you will darken mine. It hasn't been a conscious process, it has been just my natural subconscious expression that has worked out at last to a rejection of the idea that I am in love with you. Loving you means being dominated by the Oxboroughs, Morisons, Mansons, parsons' wives, Fairfields, all the base, limited, comic and timid and ugly spirits. No. I'll stick by you in most essential things but I'm not going on pretending that you are my happiness maker, my pride, my hope, my necessity. 'Votion has been asung. The Panther and the Jaguar are beasts of two different species and the Jaguar's natural habitat is up cheerful trees. I expect when I get well away I shall begin to dream again of that dear Panther I loved, who was to be of an incomparable courage, who was to be my love mate and happiness mate, who was to succeed gallantly, who was to continually increase the tale of our happy memories together, who was to make a great history with me. Until sundry landladies, cook-generals and nurses said No. But here is the reality.[3]

Wells's charges, of course, were quite unfair. Rebecca's agitation over having sent Anthony to a place not of safety but of danger was natural enough. The list of *bêtes noirs* that Wells offers is a strange one, including as it does loyal and sympathetic servants like Morison and Anthony's former nurse Emily Oxborough as well as Rebecca's disapproving mother and sisters. Rebecca later commented on Wells's "epistolary flights from the truth" of which this is a sample:

H. G. when he wrote letters to me was a different person from the one who spoke to me. He was always much more reasonable when he was with me than when he wrote to me. I can hardly remember any actual scenes taking place between us, I can hardly bring to mind one occasion when we raised our voices to each other, but when he wrote to me he was possessed by this curious irrational frenzy.[4]

At any rate, Rebecca has Rose Aubrey, her counterpart in *The Fountain Overflows,* confess: "it is not my nature to meet rage with anything but rage," [5] and she seems to have met Wells's tirade with an equally bitter reply. In her anger she wrote that she had not loved him for a year. She protested as well against the position to which Wells's arrangements had reduced her. She was a recognized and highly paid writer, fully capable of supporting herself and Anthony, but the turbulence that Wells had brought into her life made it impossible for her to work. The £2,000 in bearer bonds that he had given her the previous year was in any event a hopelessly inadequate provision for her future. Wells replied with the assurance that

> if I'm not going to be your lover I'm going to be your very loving brother. We have told each other some rather astonishing truths. Now let us keep all the appearances going for a time, a little time anyhow, before we change anything more. I'm ill and you're in a state of troubled emotions. It is quite evident that neither you nor I know at the present time how much love there is still in this. For me it means the end of love. Lusts, excitement and pretty-pretty may still get hold of me but you have been as sweet and great and beautiful a thing in my life—with all your faults carefully stated as per previous letter—as I am ever likely to meet. I shall make the World State my mistress and love that.[6]

By the end of the month the quarrel had blown over. "So long as you sticks to me," he told Rebecca, "I sticks to you."[7] And in another day or two he was able to joke about their differences:

> Interim Report of the Special Committee of
> one sitting . . . on Panther
>   after four years deliberations
> Never in the whole world has there been anyone

so sweet, so adorable, so various, so wonderful,
so consistently dear and beautiful as my Panther.

signed

Jaguar [8]

Wells's letter to Rebecca of mid-September has
been quoted at length because it is the first to bring
out the darker side of what has thus far seemed a
predominantly happy relationship. For Wells, indeed, their life together *was* essentially happy. To
have a beloved young mistress as well as an agreeable home rounded out his existence very nicely. "I
have all the money I want to spend," he told his literary agent in declining to consider a trip to America,
"my family is reasonably provided for, my life is one
of easy work, modest dignity and considerable
amusement." [9] For Rebecca the case was more complex. No doubt she felt both passion and deep affection for Wells; they suited each other as lovers, and
when in good health and temper he was the most
delightful of companions. Moreover she took pride
in the fact that he was unmistakably a great man.
But Wells was fifty and in uncertain health. He was
becoming increasingly self-centered, and he was
often restive, unreliable, and irascible. Rebecca's misgivings were strongest when they were apart, and
she could not help brooding both over what she had
to endure and what she had given up. Instead of the
full and exciting life in the center of English literary
society that might have been hers, she was spending
her youth virtually in hiding, always in a false position, always having to act a part.

Moreover, the picture offered by Wells's other life at Easton Glebe could not but present itself to her mind's eye. As Wells allowed Jane's desires to override their arrangements, as he proudly reported Gip's boyish sayings and doings, Rebecca's indignation mounted. Easton Glebe did not in itself arouse her envy. Her idea of magnificence had been formed on Abbotsford, as might have been expected of a Scottish child, and in any event as a socialist writer she disapproved of conspicuous consumption. Yet the contrast between Wells's large and comfortable house at Easton with its staff of loyal and well-trained servants, its lively and open family life, and its flow of interesting guests, in fact all of the attractions caught so pleasantly in the pages of *Mr. Britling Sees It Through,* and the domestic discomfort and humiliation made inevitable by her own irregular situation was not lost upon her. Above all she resented not so much Jane, whom she had hardly seen except during her visit to Little Easton Rectory in 1912, as the idea of Jane. Why should this woman not only share that public part of Wells's life from which she was herself excluded, and be held up to her implicitly as an example in all sorts of trivial yet irritating ways, but also pretend to the world to regard his relationship with Rebecca as a fixed grievance, when in fact she had accepted it from the first? In Rebecca's eyes Jane was a hypocrite and Easton Glebe a whited sepulchre.

Rebecca had not lost the tragic view of life which she had formed in early youth. For her these things cut deep; they were haunting spectres of the mind. She came to see Jane as that false goddess, the

Virgin Mother, the nonsexual woman to whom she as the sexual woman was being sacrificed. She felt that Wells himself, all unknowingly, was being split and destroyed by his divided allegiance to two women and two families. Presumably she told Wells very little of this. He would not admit complaints about Jane, and he insisted that she stay within her role of young mistress. But as a novelist there was another resource open to her. She wrote *The Return of the Soldier*.[10]

This story, whose conception owes as much to D. H. Lawrence as its technique owes to Henry James, is not directly about Wells and Rebecca. Wells in no way resembles Christopher Baldry, the returned soldier. Indeed, almost as if to make sure that there should be no mistake on this point, a passing reference is included to "Bert Wells, nephew to Mr. Wells who keeps the inn at Surly Hall," a cockney "bounder" whose "larking" with Margaret Allington causes Chris some annoyance.[11] Neither is Rebecca at all like Margaret, Chris's early love, nor even the narrator Jenny, who has spent her life adoring him. Instead Wells's two wives, Isabel and Jane, and what they stood for in his life have provided Rebecca's theme. She later wrote:

> H. G.'s real love was his first wife. But it was impossible that she should go on being his wife, she was not intellectual, and she was unadaptable. But she had the human qualities he valued, and he never lost his sense of shame that he had repudiated her, though it was necessary that he should do so if he were to be himself. He

was frightened of his second wife, who repre-
sented gentility to him, but it was not a happy
marriage, otherwise he would not have had all
those love affairs, and he wished he was still
with his first wife.[12]

When *The Return of the Soldier* opens in 1916,
Chris, the splendid and worshipped master of
Baldry Court, is still in France. His regular letters to
his wife Kitty have ceased during the past two weeks.
As she waits in his immaculate country house which
she has filled with rare and beautiful objects and
which she runs with clock-like precision, the house
where Chris's happiness before the war had seem-
ingly been marred only by the death of his little son,
she is visited by Margaret, a ravaged, shabbily
dressed woman who tells her that Chris is in a Boulogne hospital suffering from shell shock. He has
had a loss of memory extending back fifteen years
which has caused him to telegraph for help to
Margaret rather than to her.

This strange story is confirmed by a cousin who
sees Chris in Boulogne. He has forgotten entirely
about Kitty and their ten-year marriage. When he is
reminded that she is "a beautiful little woman" with
"a charming and cultivated soprano voice," he replies "very fractiously, 'I don't like little women and I
hate everybody, male or female, who sings. O God, I
don't like this Kitty. Take her away.' And then he
began to rave again about this [Margaret]. He said
that his body and soul were consumed with desire
for her and that he would never rest until he once
more held her in his arms." [13] When he comes

home, the sight of his wife's "serene virginity" fails to move him. "He was thinking of another woman, another beauty." [14] He still wants only to see Margaret.

The night of his return he tells Jenny of his love for Margaret at the age of twenty-one, the period of his life to which his concussion has returned him. She was the daughter of the man who kept the Monkey Island inn, a simple, direct, affectionate girl. Their love-idyll in the solitude of Monkey Island had been nearly perfect until he was called out of England by a family business crisis during what otherwise would have been a passing quarrel. He could not find Margaret on his return, and a few years later he married Kitty.

Jenny seeks out Margaret at "Mariposa, Ladysmith Road, Wealdstone," where she lives "drearily married" on a squalid back street, and brings her, as dingy as ever, to Baldry Court.[15] She has by this time come to see the warmth and vitality that lie beneath Margaret's battered exterior, but she still feels that Chris cannot but be repelled once he sees Margaret in the exquisite frame of Baldry Court. Instead they take up their love where it had been broken off. Jenny reflects:

> Chris was not mad. It was our peculiar shame that he had rejected us when he had attained to something saner than sanity. His very loss of memory was a triumph over the limitations of language which prevent the mass of men from making explicit statements about their spiritual relationships. . . . By the blankness of those eyes which saw me only as a disregarded play-

mate and Kitty not at all save as a stranger who
had somehow become a decorative presence in
his home and the orderer of his meals he let us
know completely where we were.[16]

Kitty cannot accept the peace that Margaret has
brought to Chris, and as a last resort she summons a
famous mental specialist to Baldry Court. While he
questions Chris, Margaret discovers in talking with
Jenny that she and Kitty had both had delicate boys
who died five years ago at the age of two. She reflects, "it's as if they each had half a life." [17] Then the
doctor, who is clearly an early disciple of Freud,
makes his diagnosis.

> There's a deep self in one, the essential self, that
> has its wishes. And if those wishes are sup-
> pressed by the superficial self—the self that
> makes, as you say, efforts and usually makes
> them with the sole idea of putting up a good
> show before the neighbours—it takes its
> revenge. Into the house of conduct erected by
> the superficial self it sends an obsession. Which
> doesn't, owing to a twist that the superficial self,
> which isn't candid, gives it, seem to bear any
> relation to the suppressed wish.

Chris's obsession is to forget the later years of his
life. The suppressed wish is connected with sex, to
which he had turned "with a peculiar need." "Yes,
he was always very dependent," Margaret confirms.
". . . You can't cure him, make him happy, I mean.
All you can do is to make him ordinary." [18]
    Yet Margaret and Jenny sadly agree that Chris

Freud and psychoanalysis

must be cured; a mature man cannot live perpetually in a fantasy world without becoming a pathetic oddity. So Margaret shows him his dead boy's ball and jersey and by doing so not only brings him back to the present but dooms him to return to the trenches. Margaret and Jenny are desolated. But Kitty, whom Jenny now regards as "the falsest thing on earth," whispers with satisfaction: "He's cured! . . . He's cured!" [19]

CHAPTER VIII *The*
Advancing
Hours

Few of Wells's letters to Rebecca between the fall of 1917 and the spring of 1920 have survived. It would appear, however, that this period saw little change in his relationship with her. Though the perfect confidence of their earlier years had been destroyed, the home truths that they faced during their quarrel of September 1917 were glossed over, and their life together went on much as before. This was a busy time for Wells. During the first half of 1918 he worked in Whitehall in charge of the German Section of the Committee on Enemy Propaganda. Meanwhile, he had begun a survey of universal history. As early as August of that year he could tell Rebecca that "the *Outline* is the curse (and future glory) of my life." Until the first weekly part appeared fifteen months later *The Outline of History* did indeed absorb most of his energies, but he also fitted two novels, *Joan and Peter* and *The Undying Fire,* into his schedule. At the same time he managed to see Rebecca with some regularity at Leigh, in London,

52, ST JAMES'S COURT,

BUCKINGHAM GATE. S.W.1.

Jaguar has just & Buddha.

He has finished Alexander the great

ALEXANDER
THE GOD

If you feel inclined to run up to London
& dine on Monday send a wire saying "lunch
at 1.30 Monday" *Dorothy Ell*, &
send off Saturday afternoon.

Jag.

si Clarton

Jaguar writing *The Outline of History*

and on "little jaunts" by automobile into the countryside, though his grumbling about arrangements
did not cease. "Panfer I love being with you always,"
he wrote on one occasion. "I also love being with my
work with everything handy. I *hate* being encumbered with a little boy and a nurse, and being helpful. I hate waiting about." [1]

Of one of their excursions a memento remains in
the form of a drawing by Wells. When he inquired
of Thomas Hardy from Weymouth if they might
visit Max Gate, he received the reply: "Certainly
come and see us, and bring the lady who is as yet
only a floating nebulous bright intellectuality to me.
There is nobody I should like better to see, and my
wife likewise. Will she be angry that I have not read
The Return [of the Soldier], although I have heard
it so much and so well spoken of?" [2] They accordingly arrived at Dorchester for tea on 29 January
1919. The sketch, which appears in Rebecca's copy
of *Wessex Tales,* is thus interpreted by her:

> This drawing refers to Hardy's boasts about the
> number of Roman skeletons and sepulchral
> urns that he found when rigging the founda-
> tions of his house. The dialogue should read:
>   T. H.: So I built the house entirely on skeling-
> tons.
>   Mrs. T. H. (who was a depressed lady, very
> much as pictured): Skelingtons may be healthy
> but they ain't gay soil.
>   R. W.: Lovely, lovely!
>   H. G. (who was occasionally called Tutu):
> Pants is a humbug.

Rebecca and Wells visiting the Thomas Hardys, 29 January 1919

Rebecca remained at Leigh until the winter of 1919/20 when she moved to 36 Queen's Gate Terrace in London, a fine new flat in which everything was arranged for her comfort and convenience. Anthony, who had continued in her friend's boarding school (which was transferred to the country after the London bombing became serious), rejoined his mother at the end of the war. Nanky departed, to be replaced by Peary, an almost equally reliable nurse. The settled and equable domestic pattern that resulted from these new arrangements is suggested by this joking note:

Dear Madam.

Subject to your approval, our Mr. Wells will call on you on *Wednesday* the 10th Inst. (somewhen after 4 P.M.) bringing his little bag and case of instruments. He will stay the night if necessary and hopes to give satisfaction. On Thursday he hopes to take you to the *Young Visiters* for which *you* are getting tickets. We are Madam Your respl svts

Jaguars Ltd.[3]

At first there were difficulties in Rebecca's new situation. It was brought home to her that her years of relative isolation had left her with a certain oddity of behavior. "I was too harried to have become a smooth social operator," she afterwards reflected. "I found it difficult to give people lunch or dinner, I had lived without proper household equipment so long, I didn't know when to offer drinks or how to do things." In a paradoxical way, she was like "a nun

"Egotists!" Panther and Jaguar as rival lecturers

who comes out of the convent into the world." Yet
the social circle in which Wells and Rebecca moved
began to broaden appreciably. In much of the literary world their liaison was accepted without fuss,
they went where they pleased together, and Rebecca's trenchant and amusing talk made her quite
as welcome a companion as Wells himself. Rebecca
even gave an occasional lecture, thus beginning a
mock rivalry with Wells. Anthony showed a particular feeling for music (he could follow tunes while he
was still a baby), and when Rebecca desired that he
should receive a musical education, it seemed natural to appeal for advice to Shaw, who responded
with one of his long and lively letters. He rejected as
impracticable the notion that Rebecca might start a
musical salon, but urged that Anthony should at
once begin to receive intensive training, entering
with enthusiasm on the changes that this plan would
entail in Rebecca's household. Indeed, he decidedly
favored the idea of raising Anthony as a musician,
noting that "he will be too anarchically brought up to
have much chance as a banker." [4]

In April of 1920 Wells drove Rebecca by easy
stages to South Cornwall to stay near G. B. Stern and
her husband, Geoffrey Holdsworth. Peary and her
luggage followed by train. It was a very happy ex-
pedition, and so were two subsequent visits that
Wells paid to her. Then Rebecca had a serious accident. One evening she fell into a cistern, the man-
hole of which had inadvertently been left uncovered
by Holdsworth, a scatterbrain, just outside the door
of her farmhouse. She saved herself from drowning
by clutching the sides of the cistern, and her calls for

help were answered just as the strain on her arms was becoming unbearable. But she grazed a hand in being extricated, the wound turned septic, and the sepsis spread to her face. A six-month convalescence followed in a nursing home at nearby Redruth.

Jaguar in Czechoslovakia, 1920

Meanwhile, Wells was busy with plans for trips to Czechoslovakia, Russia, and the United States. These preoccupations, which had an abnormally inflating effect on his ego, together with his unreasonable but characteristic irritation with Rebecca for being ill, led him to find excuses for not making further visits to Cornwall. "You *poor* dear," he wrote in May. "I wish I could come down and say kind things. But I'm busy getting visas, medicines and things." Further letters to his "poor sick beast" told of his brief excursion to Czechoslovakia, where he found himself a major celebrity, and urged upon Rebecca, who was hardly in a mood to dwell on the subject, the desirability of conferring with the visiting Margaret Sanger, "a most scientific female—and a dear," about the best methods of birth control. Wells's neglect of her during this period, apart from peremptory admonitions "to get this Health of yours into order," could not but cause Rebecca to have further doubts about the stability of their relationship.[5]

●Wells's curious state of mind at this time is illustrated in *The Secret Places of the Heart,* a "dialogue novel" which among other things was intended to be an admonition to Rebecca. It tells of the last year or so in the life of a "man of genius" named Sir Richmond Hardy, who as a member of the Fuel Commission is thanklessly playing a lone hand for mankind's benefit against the selfish machinations of capital and labor alike. Sir Richmond is a lover as well as a worker, and in the shadows of his life there exists a mistress named Martin Leeds, currently living away from him in Cornwall because she has a carbuncle and doesn't want him to see her disfigured. She too is presented as "a person of considerable genius," a satirical artist "who talks almost as well as she draws." When things go well, they are "glorious companions." "She is happy, she is creative, she will light up a new place with flashes of humour, with a keenness of appreciation," Sir Richmond tells Dr. Martineau under whose guidance he is exploring "the secret places of the heart." But unhappily, "things are apt to go wrong. . . . There is constant trouble with servants; they bully her." Moreover, the respective demands of his work and hers keep pulling them apart. "As things are, Martin is no good to me, no help to me. She is a rival to my duty. She feels that. She is hostile to my duty. A definite antagonism has developed. She feels and treats fuel and everything to do with fuel as a bore. It is an attack. We quarrel on that." Sir Richmond has thought of parting with Martin, but he cannot bring himself to do so. "Any one might get hold of her if I let her down. She hasn't a tithe of the ordinary cool-headed calculation of the average woman. . . . I've got a duty to her genius. I've got to take care of her."

Then Sir Richmond falls in with a young American lady who listens enthralled while he outlines early British history as they tour southwest England together. Since her father is an oil magnate, she is even able to take an intelligent interest in fuel. They fall in love, but Sir Richmond tears himself away from her after a dialogue with the absent Martin. He imagines Martin saying to him:

> No one else will ever be so intimate with you as I am. We have quarrelled together, wept together, jested happily and jested bitterly. You have spared me not at all. Pitiless and cruel you have been to me. You have reckoned up all my faults against me as though they were sins. You have treated me at times unlovingly—never was lover treated so unlovingly as you have sometimes treated me. And yet I have your love—as no other woman can ever have it. . . .
>
> Your love has never been a steadfast thing. It comes and goes—like the wind. You are an extravagantly imperfect lover. But I have learned to accept you, as people accept the English weather.

To which he retorts:

Is *yours* a perfect love, my dear Martin, with its
insatiable jealousy, its ruthless criticism? Has the
world ever seen a perfect lover yet? Isn't it our
imperfection that brings us together in a common need?

Sir Richmond returns alone to his Fuel Commission. He pushes through a report "conceived in the
generous spirit of scientific work," which may help to
arrest the drift of western civilization toward "financial and commercial squalor and . . . social col-
lapse." But the effort is too much for him, and he
dies muttering: "Best love. . . . Old Martin. . . .
Love. . . . Work." As he lies in his coffin, Martin
appears in person for the first time in the novel. She
asks Dr. Martineau:

"What am I to do now with the rest of my life?
Who is there to laugh with me now and jest?
"I don't complain of him. I don't blame him.
He did his best—to be kind.
"But all my days now I shall mourn for him
and long for him. . . ."
She turned back to the coffin. Suddenly she
lost every vestige of self-control. She sank down
on her knees beside the trestle. "Why have you
left me?" she cried.

"Oh! Speak to me, my darling! Speak to me, I
tell you! Speak to me!"

It hardly needs to be observed that *The Secret Places
of the Heart* is not a successful book, even among
Wells's dialogue novels, a designation by which he
implied that he was not making much attempt at

ℐllustrations

The Wells family and guests (H. G. Wells, Frank Wells, Jane Wells, Ella Hepworth Dixon, Wells's cousin Ruth Neale, Gip Wells) at Easton Glebe about 1912   *Courtesy of University of Illinois*

Brig-y-don, Victoria Avenue, Hunstanton, in 1973
Courtesy of Mr. Frank Wells

Quinbury, Braughing, in 1973   *Courtesy of Mr. Frank Wells*

Two views of Easton Glebe about 1915
Courtesy of Mr. Frank Wells

Ford Madox Ford and Rebecca West about 1914   *Courtesy of University of Illinois*

Ford Madox Ford, Violet Hunt, and H. G. Wells about 1914   *Courtesy of University of Illinois*

H. G. Wells about 1915   *Courtesy of*
Mr. Frank Wells

Rebecca and Anthony West about 1916
Courtesy of Dame Rebecca West

H. G. Wells at the British
Association meeting, 1923
Courtesy of Mr. Frank Wells

Rebecca West about 1923
Courtesy of Dame Rebecca West

Rebecca and Anthony West about 1928   *Courtesy of Dame Rebecca West*

H. G. Wells at a garden party, King's College, Cambridge, 1931 *Courtesy of University of Illinois*

Rebecca West about 1932   *Courtesy of University of Illinois*

characterization or plot.[6] Still, its message for Rebecca was clear. Unluckily for Wells, Rebecca hardly received his admonitory parable as he had intended. Instead she thought it was funny; and even her mother, who usually viewed her association with Wells as tragic, was reduced by it to hopeless laughter. When Rebecca told him of this reaction, he was annoyed.

Their separation was protracted by Wells's trip to Russia during September and October. On his return they met in London. Rebecca, cured of her carbuncle but still anemic and overtired, had been ordered to Italy for the winter. She was consequently engaged in letting her flat, placing Anthony in a school run by a friend ("far too early," she was later to reflect), and arranging for Peary's welfare, before setting out for Capri. Wells himself was now experiencing a time of trouble. His health was uncertain. A hysterectomy was impending for Jane. And he was increasingly bored and dissatisfied with the life that he led as a public personage. He came to see Rebecca as his one refuge from all this turmoil.

When they met, however, there was another major quarrel. In his irritation Wells let it slip that he had been unfaithful to her with Moura Benckendorf, Maxim Gorky's secretary, a confession that at first reduced Rebecca to tears of misery,[7] though she quickly expressed a spirited determination to retaliate in kind with a handsome young man. "Please love me and be faithful to me," Wells pleaded with her in a note whose self-abnegation contrasts oddly with the brassy assurance of his letters of the previous summer:

It is much bitterer and more humiliating for
the male and I can't bear the thought of it. I
love you and want to keep you anyhow, but I
know that in spite of myself I shan't be able to
endure your unfaithfulness. I am horribly
afraid now of losing you. It will be a disaster for
both of us. It will cut the heart out of my life. I
don't think it will leave much in yours.[8]

There was a reconciliation of sorts before Rebecca
departed for Italy. Wells pursued her with contrite
letters, decorated with aloof Panthers and despon-
dent Jaguars, in which he told of the difficulties he
was having in the preparation of his American lec-
tures, the horror with which he regarded the prospect of delivering them ("Eight weeks of Americans!
My God! Why did I do IT?"), his anxiety over Jane's
condition, and his own "soul destroying cold." [9] It
was this state of mind that produced one of the most
extraordinary of his letters to Rebecca.

I am almost unendurably lonely and miserable. I've got tired. I've done no end of work and
good work. I've really changed British policy
about Russia and when I sit in judgement on
myself I smother myself with [w]reaths. The
Outline of History is going to change History.
I've done good things and big things. It doesn't
matter a damn so far as my wretchedness is concerned. Righteous self applause is not happiness. Russia excited me and kept me going. Now
I'm down. I'm alone. I'm busy. I'm tired. I want
a breast and a kind boddy, I want to be treated
kindly and to feel safe and warm and *near*. I

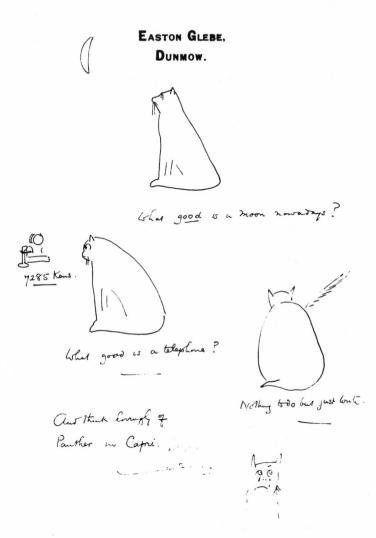

**EASTON GLEBE,
DUNMOW.**

What good is a moon nowadays?

7285 Kens.

What good is a telephone?

And think enough of
Panther in Capri.

Nothing to do but just wait.

Jaguar alone in London, 1920

want love. I want love that I can touch and feel.
And I don't deserve love. I've trampled on people. I've nagged at and bullied you. I've not kept
faith: I've almost tried to lose you. You are
probably the only person who can really give me
love and make me love back. And because
you've been ill I've treated you so's I've got no
right to you any more. I don't believe I'll find
you next April. If I don't find you then I hope
I'll find Death. I can't go on being the dull slave
of the Salvage of the World. I can't—in my
present state anyhow—bank on religion. God
has no thighs and no life. When one calls to him
in the silence of the night he doesn't turn over
and say, "What is the trouble Dear?" I'm miserable and lonely and disgusted and flat. Have I
ever got into your arms to cry? I would like to
do that now. (Though I believe we should presently forget about the crying in our mooshal efforts to comfort each other.) *Dear* Panfer. I
wonder how much this is just being cut off from
you. I don't know, but of the unexampled misery of my mind there is no doubt whatever.[10]

Wells was sustained at this time by the prospect of
joining Rebecca in Italy after his American tour, but
even this vision was clouded by doubts. Look on this
picture, and on this, he told her in effect in a letter
of late November:

Shall I certainly and truly and faithfully find a
well panfer, a *faifful* panfer, a *loving* panfer, a
bright ready kind panfer at Capri, a dear *Equal* active mate, and have happy weeks in Italy with

the dearest companion in the world, the dearest
and sweetest and happiest, scampering about,
purring, sleeping in a heap
>   or
shall I find
>   a sick distraught female, much
preoccupied about some *really* handsome man
whom she doesn't in the least love but nevertheless talks about endlessly. . . .

Orrible Jaguar I am! [11]

Not long thereafter Wells cancelled his trip to the
United States. Jane's recovery from her operation
was slow, and his cold had developed into pneumonia. His doctors told him "to write a novel or 'something easy like that' in warm and beautiful surround-
ings," [12] and Wells eagerly proposed that he set out
for Italy as soon as possible. He would be "feeble at
first," no doubt, but then "vigorous." As his strength
returned, he made urgent suggestions as to what arrangements would best provide for "a free flow of
pleasant sensuality" after his arrival. [13]

Meanwhile, Rebecca was encountering troubles of
her own on Capri. The new friend with whom she
had intended to stay for some weeks fell ill, and
Rebecca found that she was expected to stay with her
indefinitely. Since the poor lady could not be left
alone in an isolated villa, Rebecca stayed on but
wrote to her hostess's husband and brother telling
them that they must make some arrangement for
her care and that she herself must leave. Her letters
were never answered. It was three months before
she left the villa, finally resigning her charge to the

care of the neighbors. When she reached the main-
land, she was herself in a state of nervous exhaus-
tion.

About 25 January Wells joined "Miss West," his
"secretary and companion," [14] at the Hotel Cappuc-
cini in Amalfi in a particularly nervous and irritable
state of mind. He was sure that Rebecca's protracted
stay on Capri could only be explained by a love affair, and this was but one of the imaginary grievances that he had conceived during his recent
months of ill health and worry. Moreover, a
drunken old major of fiercely Tory principles became most objectionable when he found out who
Rebecca and Wells were. There was a great scandal
in the hotel, which Wells minded very much, Rebecca recalls, "and said that he did not but that I did
and I ought to conceal it from him." When an English acquaintance of Wells turned up, Wells took
out his annoyance at being discovered with Rebecca
by being particularly rude to her in front of him.
Rebecca was so depressed and humiliated as to be
touched by the smallest favors. In after years she
remembered with gratitude how an ironmonger, a
capable person later to become Mayor of Croydon,
who could talk entertainingly about the local iron
work, went out of his way together with his sister to
accompany Wells and herself to the ruins at Paes-
tum. But this display of kindness and others like it
were of no avail, because Wells would not accept
them; as soon as people began to behave cordially,
he found them bores. It was as if he wanted "to drag
her into situations where mud would be thrown at
her," Rebecca later reflected. "He wanted the rudeness, the slights, the contempt for me."

Wells and Rebecca remained in Amalfi for a month before moving north together by easy stages. When he returned to England, he thanked her for "two months and a half of almost unbroken happiness." [15] Rebecca, who stayed on the Continent until early May, by no means saw the experience in the same light, but she did not express her reservations to Wells, who sent her a series of fervent love letters. The first and the last will serve as examples:

> I shall be so glad when you are back in London. I am beginning to miss you dreadfully. I didn't at first. I was busy with coming back and all sorts of things. Now that I have settled down, I begin to want someone about who is—you. Someone to go about with, to stroll in to and scold, to go out to lunch with, to take to a movie and all the little dear companionships one hardly notices while one has them. (And there are such fings as beds.) We *were* tremendously together all that time. So hurry up with the *Mothers* and come back to some more love. And don't get too much in love with Reggie or Orioli or any of them. Because really I am better than any of them. [16]

> I love you more than any other human being. You are my dearest companion. I love and admire you. If I did not love you I should still think you one of the wisest and sweetest of human beings. You've got all sorts of superficial faults and weaknesses but the stuff of you is the best stuff I've ever met inside a human skin. (And it is lovely to have you.) I want to be with you as much as I possibly can. I love your voice.

I'm not really happy except when you are about.
I am prouder of being your "dear Jaguar" than
anything else in the world.[17]

᠂ The summer of 1921 passed uneventfully, Wells
spending part of most weeks with Rebecca at her
Queen's Gate Terrace flat. Telling her of a reunion
with "Elizabeth," who "broke into a conversation on
women writers and critics, Mrs. Belloc Lowndes,
May Sinclair, Katherine Mansfield &c. started by
Brett with violent praises of your manly vigour and
jolly wit," he hastened to add: "No carryings [on].
Jaguar still pure."[18] At this time Wells was at pains
to give Anthony something approaching a family
life. A brief surviving diary shows "Wellsie," "Auntie
Panther," "Pearie," and Anthony on motor excursions to Bath and to Hunstanton, where swimming
was the order of the day, and there is also a series of
little stories and poems with Anthony as their hero.
Both are illustrated with some of Wells's choicest
drawings.[19] Indeed, Wells was proud of his preco-
cious seven-year-old son, about whom he cautioned
Rebecca: "Don't talk about him or let Peary talk
about him, in front of him. He hears everything."[20]
    In mid-October of 1921 Wells went to the United
States alone, having failed to persuade Rebecca to
accompany him. From the S.S. *Adriatic* he sent her a
series of chatty love letters, written out of a "brain
bored flat," so he put it, "by American talk and
American want of ideas, by strangers, by the lack of
any sane sweet satisfying companionship." "If I have
much more of this bloody steamship," he remarked
two days out from New York, "I shall begin to write

We went to Sherringham in the Albert car.

You can see Wellsie driving and Auntie Panther beside him and me and Pearie and Dowie behind

The sand was lovely and there were lots of people bathing but I did not go in.

I ate an Ice.

August 1. 1921

Good Boy.

Seaside excursion, sketched for Anthony, 1 August 1921

There was once a featless Cow Boy named.
N-___-Ni. in the Indian language or in
English, Antony.   And as he came out of
the Far West, he was called Antony West.

And   he   lassoed   a   Deinotherium
(like the ones in Wellsie's book)   And

Wellsie came along and put it in his Book
And that is how it came to be in his Book.

september 14 1921   Good Night

Anthony as a cowboy, 14 September 1921

' like Dorothy Richardson." All that sustained him was the expectation of his reunion with Rebecca in Spain. He promised her that he would not be ill, as in Italy the previous winter, and he urged her to finish *The Judge,* the novel on which she was working. "I want dear Panfer with a fresh mind biting on a new world with a sense *of something triumphantly finished.*" [21]

Wells's mission in the United States was to report the Washington Peace Conference for the *New York World* and the *Chicago Tribune,* an assignment for which he received $50,000. These papers saw to it that everywhere he went a blaze of "publicity" accompanied him. "I am really famous here," he discovered, "people turn round in the street and when I went to a play by and for coloured people the other night the house stood up and clapped." He was entertained constantly, he met the celebrities of the day, and he was comfortably accommodated in the Tom Lamonts' "very sumptuous and quiet house in New York" and at the Cosmos Club in Washington. Near the end of his stay he noted: "I've worked hard here and fairly well and I think I've pulled my full weight in a big and necessary tug." [22] Yet all the while Wells longed for Rebecca's company, even arguing, somewhat illogically in view of his status as a famous man, that "we've exaggerated the blackmail possibilities." He wrote:

> It is curious how warmly and friendly I love you nowadays. It isn't at all the raw desire and fits of hate and devotion of new passion, but it's an extraordinary longing to have you about mixed up

COSMOS CLUB
WASHINGTON, D. C.

"No letter from Panther," 19 November 1921

with a real intellectual need to gossip with you
(nobody talks better than print over here) and a
mass of gross desires for your thighs and your
arms and the corner of your mouf. Be a *good*
panfer. Not to be kissed or flattered too much.
You've got me and that's what you want.[23]

CHAPTER IX *Dusty Answer*

Rebecca met Wells at Gibraltar on 17 January 1922, leaving Anthony at Queen's Gate Terrace with Peary, and they went immediately to the Maria Cristina in Algeciras. But the reunion, from which Wells had hoped for so much, proved to be a disastrous failure. He was in no better health or spirits than he had been the year before in Italy. The rigors of American travel had exhausted him, and the excesses of American adulation had left him in a dangerously exalted frame of mind. The Maria Cristina was a conservative English establishment, more a club than a hotel, but he behaved there as if he were a "conquering hero," quite above normal proprieties.

The day after his arrival he contracted a sore throat. Finding that the local doctor was away, he demanded first of Rebecca and then of the proprietors of the hotel that they phone the Admiral of the Fleet at Gibraltar for a naval doctor, saying that "of course the Admiral would realise that he must do all he could if H. G. was ill." A retired doctor was found in the foothills behind Algeciras who said that a mild gargle would meet the needs of the case, but Wells remained convinced that he was mortally afflicted. For days Rebecca, herself in poor health and sick at heart at the renewal of the familiar pattern, was in constant attendance on him in his sick room, even having to confine her meals to fruit and sandwiches since he could not bear the noise of spoons and forks on china.

When Wells finally got up, his "love of scenes became a mania." Everywhere they went, he forced Rebecca to play out painful public dramas as "the ill-treated mistress" of a man twice her age. He would ask her "to go and fetch his coat in front of a number of people, which in a Latin country went very badly indeed." "The proprietor of the Hotel Maria Cristina," Rebecca continues, "came to me and told me that if I had not the fare to get home he and his wife would give me it and they would get me passage on a boat and smuggle me over to Gibraltar. In Seville the English chaplain and his wife asked if they could not wire to my relatives in England to come and fetch me." Matters went better in this city, however, for there Wells and Rebecca fell in with Pat Dansey and Joan Campbell, two middle-aged ladies whose native wit was reinforced by wealth and aristocratic birth. They were not to be overawed by Wells and kept him in order during their stay.

Rebecca was nonetheless eager to get Wells away from Seville, where his behavior had been particularly rude and eccentric. Miss Dansey and Miss Campbell proposed Granada, which they knew well, but Wells, after first agreeing, suddenly said he would not go because "Arab civilisation in Spain was only a low form of civilisation not worthy of his consideration." He changed his mind when Rebecca in her astonishment called him "a pompous schoolmaster," a description he never forgot, and indeed Granada turned out to be a distinct improvement since the hotel was quiet and empty of English visitors. Even here, however, Wells "walked out half way through a party given to him, with dancers laid on and local poets, by Manuel de Falla." Madrid provided a peaceful interlude, but Paris was again a disaster. When they could not find their small hotel on returning from a walk, Wells rebuked Rebecca, explaining that it was her "duty as a custodian of genius to know that sort of thing." He refused to take her to see Anatole France, because she was "not goodlooking enough." Rebecca came to feel that "he was utterly out of gear with reality, a sick man."

By mid-March, when Wells left for England, Rebecca was giving serious thought to asserting her independence. How long, she asked herself, could she be expected to continue as a virtual nurse, to the total interruption of her own work? How Wells saw their situation may be judged from a letter he wrote to Rebecca on 20 March:

> The old male Pusted [i.e. cat] has read her letter attentively and declines to plead guilty to an Enlarged Egotism. He objects to the Better Jaguar Movement.
> The Better Panther Movement (nagging schoolmaster) was dropped before the Italian holiday. It had only one revival when Jaguar in-

sisted upon having that book finished before the
Spanish holiday. It is now dead altogether. Panther can be, do and act as she damn pleases.
Jaguar proposes no further comments—only resistance or non participation when he personally
is involved. He thinks the Better Jaguar Movement had better follow the Better Panther
Movement *tout suite.*

The old male Pusted does not care a damn
about any Scandal except in so far as it distresses
her imagination. That sort of Mook Scandals
anyhow. He does not care how things strike people.

He went to Granada after all to please her. It
pleased him but that he did not know before-
hand.

He funked 48 hours on the train because she
does not travel well and neither of them were in
the mood for much mutual helpfulness. A Scandal about Madrid or Paris would not have hurt
her; it would have smashed up his political influence (such as it is) upon the Franco British
situation.

The above sort of argey-bargey is a bore.

The old male Pusted will henceforth treat the
young female Pusted with a courtly politeness.
He will, so help him, never ask her to fetch his
coat downstairs or any such insulting service
again. A barrier of respect shall be set up between them. If the projected Better Jaguar
Movement goes on he will receive its intimations
with attention but he does not propose to treat
them as commands. And when he does not feel

up to being improved by Panther and her
Friends he will just have to keep away.[1]

But in fact these rather surly concessions met only
Rebecca's surface grievances. She had been reflecting profoundly on her situation, indeed she had
even put her difficulties to Wells's lawyer friend
George Whale. When she later stated her case
against Wells, her bill of particulars was as follows:

> that he treated me with the sharpest cruelty
> imaginable for those horrible years, that he hu-
> miliated me . . . that he overworked me and
> refused to allow me to rest when I was ill, that
> he has cheated me of all but one child, that his
> perpetual irascibility ruined my nerves, that he
> isolated me and drove away my friends.[2]

Nonetheless, Rebecca and Wells arrived at a reconciliation which endured for a time, despite its evident instability. Their spring holiday together was
"perfect," or so Wells at least believed, and he continued to see her on the old terms during the early
summer. Meanwhile, he was attempting "to start a
sort of English review" with Rebecca as editor and
himself as advisor and patron. It was to be named *La
Belle Sauvage,* and there was to be "a naked Panther
with a club in an oval on the cover and a section (edi-
torial) called *Cracking their Bones* with Panfer (nood)
in her Cave as a headpiece."[3] Once successfully
launched, Wells told Rebecca, "it will give you a safe
income and a considerable margin of time to get out
your own creative work."[4] Rebecca had no faith in
what she later called "this typical piece of Wellsery."

Her literary position was already established. Commissions came to her as she needed them. Even if she had believed in Wells's business capacity, which she did not, she would never have consented "to live in a box" to which only he had the key.

In late July Wells drove Rebecca and Anthony to Porlock, a picturesque village on the Somerset shore of the Bristol channel, returning himself to London almost at once. The "work impulse" was strong in him, and Rebecca had not urged him to stay, since the inn, run by a "vinegary spinster," was "too respectable" for them "to be easy and happy." When letters from her did not arrive regularly, however, he began to brood over the "little friends" with whom he had left her: the Holdsworths (G. B. Stern and her husband), young Hugh Hart, Rebecca's sister Letty, and Richard O'Sullivan. Rebecca was very fond of Mrs. Holdsworth, who at this time badly needed companionship since her husband's hold on sanity was becoming precarious. Rebecca later described Hart as "a very cultivated and rather spiritless Jewish business man, and amateur musician," in love with a married woman. Rebecca had known him since she was eighteen. O'Sullivan, a Catholic like Letty, was an Irish barrister of exemplary character, loyal to a mad wife. A less riotous group could hardly have been assembled; but, after Jane and her sons left for a Swiss holiday, Wells in his loneliness became increasingly suspicious and resentful of Rebecca.

His second visit to Porlock was a total disaster. He arrived miserable with fatigue. When his energy returned, he and Rebecca set off on an automobile trip that turned into a comedy of errors. Rebecca was later to recollect:

> We drove all over Somerset and Devon one day. He refused to stop at any inn for lunch because they all looked wrong. When he settled on one it was too late and there was a row because they would not serve us. Finally we settled in for the night at a curious inn right in the middle of a barren moor, near a place which I think was called Box. This was kept by a man who was obviously going out of his mind and who lived there alone with his despairing daughter. I think this man had bought the inn on some gratuity he got at the end of a term in the colonial service. Anyway nobody was coming to the inn, which seemed natural enough as there was not a soul in sight, the nearest village was miles away. Someone else arrived, a commercial traveller, and H. G. and the landlord and the commercial traveller played some three-handed game of cards for a whole day, and the daughter and I sat in the kitchen and she wept and we did household chores together. Then H. G. took me back to Porlock and went off in a huff.

After his return to London Wells gave free vent to his jealousy.[5] "I don't believe the Porlock affair just happened," he told Rebecca. "It was fixed up by you and the Holdsworths to give you a time with Hart." And he continued in another letter:

> As I see it I was squeezed out of that while you had Hart there and your sister had her lover. I

don't know how far things went. I know you tol-
erate enormous familiarities from the Holdsworths. No doubt this is unjust and so forth.
The thing that matters is the emotional
estrangement. I *detest* Holdsworths. Either you
clean up that corner and get rid of this irritating
follower or you lose any intimacy with me. It's
no good starting a *tu quoque*.

Wells later admitted that his accusations were un-
founded and unworthy, yet his instinct was not entirely at fault, since in fact Rebecca's friends were
urging her to break with him.

As the quarrel continued by letter, Wells chose as
his chief point of attack the harm that Rebecca's intimacy with the Holdsworth circle was doing to her
work. From the beginning of their association he
had been at odds with Rebecca's passionate convic-
tions concerning the importance of art in all its
forms. Though they had managed to avoid a dispute
over Henry James, Wells's *Boon* and Rebecca's little
book on the Master, which appeared in 1915 and
1916 respectively, are poles apart in their assump-
tions. Emphasizing this difference, Wells now told
Rebecca that in the *New Statesman,* where she provided a sympathetic and wide-ranging commentary
on the art, literature, and theatre of the day, she was
praising just the authors she should be attacking, no
doubt prompted by her "little friends." Moreover,
her novel *The Judge* was "an ill conceived sprawl of a
book with a faked hero and a faked climax, an
aimless waste of your powers." With an air of high-
minded candor which must have been an additional
provocation to Rebecca, he continued:

I've tried to let you down easily about the *Judge*
but I feel that if we are to go on you've got to
have exactly what I think of it. The book is to[o]
important in our lives. If we are to have suppressed opinions about it—or on your part
about my books—the irritation of the suppres-
sion will destroy any sort of mental community.
I've got no use for you at all as a humbugged
pet woman. If I am going to have a female pet I
could get any number of prettier and more
amusing pets than you. With us it is either complete companionship or nothing.

A formal separation seemed to impend, though
Wells hoped that knowledge of it could be kept from
the world for a time. He continued his efforts to
being *La Belle Sauvage* into being, seeing it as an
outlet which would free Rebecca from the literary
circle whose influence he deplored. And he con-
fessed that behind the touchiness which had recently
made him so disagreeable lay profound dissatis-
factions of his own with their relationship:

I am very sorry if this storm has distressed you.
I have been unhappy for four years. Except for
the Pusted-Fido business you have given me no
love and no help for a very long time. I wanted
to see if you thought there was anything worth
making a fight for between our minds. Manifestly you don't think there is. You let me go.

The break for a time seemed final, and Wells was
no doubt sincere when he told Rebecca "we are out
of love with each other and the poor panguar is

dead and torn to pieces." Yet in fact there were still powerful forces holding the two together. Even Wells's letters of recrimination were dotted with tributes to "some sort of Rebecca West who isn't like this, I love her passionately now, a wise kind and adorable lover." And as his rage subsided, he wrote to her in increasingly conciliatory terms. If they could only meet and talk, he maintained, most of their troubles "would vanish like a nightmare when one wakes." He glanced back over their life together:

We've had a love and friendship so dear and good that it wasn't good enough. We've been the dearest friends and lovers and we have afflicted and attacked and encumbered each other all the time. This last journey to Cornwall was full of such dear and delightful things. Whenever we have been free together and alone together I have been happy. Our spring holiday was perfect to me. Thetford, the sands beyond Hunstanton, much of Braughing, that deep flooded ditch there where we waded, Gladys in those days, the Leigh flats, the air raids we shared, Monkey Island,—and Claverton afternoons. And all the while we have been fighting against each other—discontents—contentions. Seeing it was so near perfect why didn't we and why don't we now make it perfect? Because it's just about that that we always quarrel. Our ways of work and a lot of our personal habits are incompatible, ungracious warrings. My memories of you run in two sets but the greatest set is truly you, my Panther, dignified and wise and dear.

In another of his letters analysis took the place of nostalgia.

It seems to me that almost fundamental in this trouble is something I should call *Drive*. It's not the same thing as energy because my Drive goes on when I am worked out, producing friction, bad temper, things like this outbreak. It says everlastingly oh *Get on* with it! It is a race against death. It's what you mean when you called me—never mind, we've done with that. It's what I am—I can't help it! You, I don't think, have Drive as I have. Your interest in things, so vivid, so adorable and discursive, so that now you throw light on Spain, on a book, on some poor drab of an unsuccessful actress, on a crime, on riding horses—which I always regarded with scorn and contempt until you took to it—well it's just what the Drive won't permit. . . .

Nothing I think will ever cure this fundamental difference between us. We have always gone along with this discordance and any life we share in the future will have the same discordance. I don't think it affects the fact that I love you, honour you, revere you, bow down before the beauty of your spirit and the beauty of your personality, your kindness, profound honesty—all you are. All the love I bear you will never prevent the disposition to damn at—an hour's sleep snatched in the morning or the evening spent in talking to a young man like Hart.

I think therefore you are wise in setting about as you are doing to save the rest of your life from me. Your decision is my infinite loss but it will not be a fatal loss. I don't feel deeply. I curse and swear and spend sleepless nights wandering about the house or doing work and I drowse during the day. I shall get on with it all right and you have no obligation to me. "Consolations" will come fast enough. And if I can be any sort of friend or companion to you I shall be glad. Do realize that though I can curse you, be unfaithful to you as I was in Russia, goad you and scold you, abuse your work, bring fantastically absurd (self tormenting) charges of unfaithfulness against you and so and so on—you have the catalogue—nevertheless I love you intensely. You have the most wonderful brain I have ever met, the sweetest heart, the most loving and delightful humour, wit abounding, on ten thousand occasions you have been supremely beautiful to me—

Nevertheless I think you are wise to disentangle the rest of your life from mine.[6]

Wells's arguments against himself had the effect which he intended. Against her better judgment, Rebecca fell back into her old relationship with him.

CHAPTER X **Falcons**
in a Snare

The winter of 1922/23 passed without special incident, but in March an announcement that Rebecca was to lecture in the United States led to "an attempt on the part of an American clubwoman to get her held up at Ellis Island for immorality," which was "foiled by a New York lawyer." This development led her to reconsider her position with some urgency.[1] George Whale had already suggested a demand that Wells leave Jane and marry her as the only possible solution to Rebecca's problem. Marriage was not a step that she herself regarded as either feasible or desirable. Early in their relationship, she had dismissed the possibility in a letter which Wells destroyed along with the rest of her correspondence. Rebecca later recalled:

> I said that I thought he was rooted in his domestic routine, that I was sure he felt there was something right about it, that I saw well that Jane's friends would make life impossible, and

that I recognised that it would be hard on the
two sons.

Yet nothing could prevent the fact of Jane's existence from impinging disastrously on Wells's life
with her.

> As time went on my attitude was "If Jane is per-
> fect, why don't you go back to her and if you
> don't will you please refrain from criticising me
> because my house is not as comfortable as hers?"
> But sometimes as he wouldn't go back to Jane
> and leave me, I did say to him, "Well, we can't
> go on like this, the situation is getting worse and
> worse."

Moreover, as Anthony grew older Rebecca was
sometimes made to feel that life with Wells was becoming impossible without marriage.

> One day H. G. came in when I was out and
> found the housekeeper was going to fetch An-
> thony from his school and bring him back to
> lunch, and he said he would go instead, and did,
> with the consequence that I got a grossly insult-
> ing letter from the headmistress saying that she
> was already defying convention in having An-
> thony in the school and this appearance of H. G.
> might have caused a scandal so I had better re-
> move Anthony. Not unnaturally when I got the
> letter I cried, and when I told H. G. why I was
> crying he flew into a passion.

At any rate, when rumors of the Boston clubwoman's campaign reached Rebecca through Letty,

they proved to be the last straw. Appalled at the
danger to her reputation that they seemed to fore-
bode, not to mention the accompanying threat to her
earning power, she told Wells that they must marry
or separate permanently. She did this, however, in
the confident expectation that he would not divorce
Jane and that their relationship would consequently
be terminated.

Wells's immediate response was a brusque, angry
letter, apparently written in the hope of overriding
Rebecca's arguments:

> I am sorry about this Boston fuss. Something
> of the sort happens about most people who go
> to America. But I don't think it fair for you to
> turn on me with this growing mania of yours
> about the injustice of my treatment of you in not
> murdering Jane. The thing goes on and on with
> you and I am tired to death of it. I do regret
> very bitterly that I ever met you but I have done
> what I could to make some sort of tolerable life
> for us. I can do no more than I have done. It's
> your business, in my idea, to disregard these
> fool scandals and go to America and succeed, as
> you certainly will do if you go, in spite of them.
> It's not your business, it's not playing the game,
> to lacerate me about it. For ten years I've shaped
> my life mainly to repair the carelessness of one
> moment. It has been no good and I am tired of
> it.[2]

When Rebecca remained adamant, Wells proposed terms for their separation. Anthony was to be

left entirely in her hands with Wells paying his
school bills. Rebecca was to receive £500 a year until
she married or was "otherwise associated with a
man." But along with these suggested arrangements,
Wells offered apologies and excuses for past of-
fenses, arguments against his divorcing Jane, renewed protestations of his love for Rebecca, and
suggestions that a reconciliation was still possible:

> We parted like lovers on Tuesday morning
> and you exploded into rage and hate in the af-
> ternoon. And it is just as if all the fun, endear-
> ment, tenderness, friendliness and love of ten
> years had not been. You want no more of it and
> neither do I. You never want to see me again
> and I do not want to come back to you. I regret
> an enormous failure and ten years of your life
> and ten years of mine. But I want to say plainly
> to you that I will not accept any imputation that
> I have treated you badly or broken any promise
> to you. . . . I have done my utmost to love you
> and I would have come to you and lived with
> you under any circumstances that would not
> have wrecked my work. I may have made things
> difficult for you but you have never made things
> easy for me. I don't think you realize how dif-
> ficult it has been at times to play the lover to
> you.
> But anyhow, now that you are quit of me and
> the inconvenience of my presence near you, I
> want to see you succeed. You have all the mak-
> ings of a success still before you, you are young

enough to heal up from this forced love of ours
and care for other people and wipe out your unpleasant memories of the last ten years. You are
a much more attractive person than you were
ten years ago. I do not love you and I do not
feel the slightest stirring of jealousy about you
but I do feel the very greatest admiration and
friendliness for you.

———————

I admit I have been negligent of your comfort
and honour. I have grown more prosperous and
conspicuous and I've just not bothered to read-
just. I admit the extreme selfishness of that. But
it isn't that I've been lavishing my accumulations
elsewhere. They've just accumulated. I do not
see why you should not have a comfortable
home in the country with two or three servants
and real comfort, where I can live with you most
of our time, why you should not have a little flat
of your own in London and why our friends
shouldn't recognize each other instead of this icy
mutual ignoring of each other. That tune was
set by your mother. There is no earthly need to
keep it on now.

Will you ask yourself if you love me, and if
you do will you do this for me, will you try to
make a common life for us possible? . . .

Consider what sort of life you would get with
me before and after the divorce. Jaguar in possession of his Panther again, press cuttings of
the divorce proceedings coming in, all his work
disorganized—obliged to attend himself to his
translation business, his income tax returns, do-

mestic bills, banking accounts. No alternative to our beautiful little new home. He'd be the darlingest little Jaguar. And Panther too might find Jane's captured wedding ring not nearly so magic in compelling servants and the world to respect as she imagined. Then of course she would take it out of Jaguar again. He'd got the divorce too late. He'd got it in the wrong way. He'd engaged the wrong sort of cook. And so on and so on.[3]

When these maneuvers failed, Wells still had his trump card to play: the appeal from self-abnegation which had always pulled him through before. It came in the last letter of this significant series.

You know you must face certain facts about me. It is a most important thing for you to understand how persistently I doubt the possibility of anyone loving me. I dislike myself as an inadequate instrument. I am maddened by my fluctuations of will and mood. I think I am ill looking. I am not amused at myself in any way. I cannot understand anyone loving me. I can understand you being intensely loved or my boys being loved. But not this hard, strained inconsistent thing with a sort of greatness and a voice and a life that jangles.

I want you to save the rest of your life from me, but do let me help you in every possible way to keep your life dignified and free. I *will* come to the flat when you return and we can surely come to an understanding on these matters. I rebel against you, I try to get rid of you, but I love you and also I respect you. I'm not really a Jaguar or a Pusted or a Fido or any of the dear things I have loved to pretend to be. I am a man who has had the dearest most wonderful love and has requited it ill. But I do now want to help and sustain your life as well as I can. Don't tear up the flat and throw the pieces at me because I had something to do with it. And if the Jaguar you created vanishes there remains a man you don't understand who cares for you and worships you as well as insulting and raging and beating at you. He's done these things, insults and rage and so on, for the last time since you dismiss him but he will work with you if he can.

I don't know Panther. I haven't the face to ask you to try again. If we try again you will be you and I shall be I. We may have learnt a mutual consideration but it is foolish to make promises. We shall love and we shall jar. You say the love isn't worth the torment of the discord.

Leave it at that.[4]

Rebecca did not yield entirely. She kept her distance from Wells, but without any open disavowal of him. This complicated their lives considerably, since their friends were in the habit of asking them everywhere as a couple. When they joined forces to entertain the Sinclair Lewises in April, Wells found his new status humiliating. His complaints were piteous:

Last night was unexpectedly painful. I don't think I want to meet you any more or be re-

minded very much about you. I've been hanging
on so far because I suppose at the back of my
mind was a persuasion that you loved me
enough to come back to me and that we could
then fix a way of living that wouldn't wound
you. But you've changed already. I don't want to
watch the change go on to its manifest end.
Apart from anything else I don't think you realize the enormous pride I had in you and the humiliation it was to see Sinclair Lewis slobber his
way up your arm—and to think that was going
on, that sort of thing to a real life of Freedom.
My Panther.[5]

This letter infuriated Rebecca, who loathed Lewis
and had been revolted by his attentions, yet she
might once again have relented as in the past but for
an episode which convinced her that a final break
with Wells was inevitable.

In the winter of 1922/23, restless and *désoeuvré* as a
result of his uncertain relations with Rebecca, Wells
allowed himself to become deeply involved with Frau
Hedwig Verena Gatternigg, a young Austrian journalist. His awareness of this lady, at least through
correspondence, extended back for some time. Wells
saw her mother, Frau Duchinsky, on several occasions when she visited London in the summer of
1922,[6] and her intervention seems to have paved the
way for a meeting with Frau Gatternigg when she in
turn came to the city in the fall. Against his usual
practice, Wells even gave her an interview for her
"American syndicate," and took the trouble to cor-
rect the text that she sent to him.[7]

*Given Frau Gatternigg's evident instability, Wells would ordinarily have kept away from her, but at this juncture his irritation with Rebecca seems to have weakened his defenses. The newspapers later described her as "an attractive and pretty young woman, small, with petite features, dark hair and big brown eyes with long curling lashes," who was about twenty-eight years old and spoke English perfectly. This account, as we shall learn, is not confirmed by Rebecca, but if it is taken to represent Wells's impression of her, his behavior becomes more comprehensible. She wrote to him asking to be allowed to describe the plight of the educated classes in Vienna, and he invited her to tea with Jane and himself at Whitehall Court. At this and other meetings he learned that she was the daughter of a professor, who admired his writings on education, and the wife of a naval officer, and that she had come to England on the rebound from an unhappy love affair with a Secretary at the British Embassy in Vienna. Wells authorized her to translate *The Great Schoolmaster,* a book on Sanderson of Oundle which he was in the process of completing, and this commission provided a pretext for further visits to Whitehall Court during which less and less attention was paid to the problems of translation. The two even spent a passionate weekend together near Easton Glebe, where Frau Gatternigg was conveniently looking after the house of some absent friends. When she returned to the Continent later in the winter, Wells provided her fare to Austria and an introduction to Anatole France in which he described her as "a very interesting and intelligent young Austrian (speaking French

very well) who will give you my love and tell you all
sorts of curious and interesting things about
Vienna." [8]

Frau Gatternigg came back to London in June,
eager to resume the affair, but by this time Wells's
ardor had cooled. Among the expedients which he
adopted to put her off was a suggestion that she see
Rebecca, who was planning a trip to Marienbad. Rebecca retains a vivid memory of their meeting:

> She presented herself at my flat on the morning
> of June 20, with a letter of introduction from
> H. G. Her manner was so peculiar that Peary felt
> suspicious of her when she opened the door to
> her and showed her in, and when she brought
> coffee to us she was so puzzled by the woman's
> behaviour that she went down several flights of
> stairs to see if the policeman was on point duty
> at the end of the street in case she had to call
> him.
>
> I had no suspicion of anything being out of
> the way about her relations with H. G. . . . She
> was a plain woman, small and thin, and I should
> have said in her middle thirties, not at all
> coquettishly dressed, with a withered hand and
> arm. She had a strong Austrian accent—of this I
> am quite sure, as she rang me up a number of
> times during the next ten or fifteen years.
>
> H. G. was not mentioned at all between us
> after I had read the letter of introduction, ex-
> cept in the briefest manner. Frau Gatternigg
> pressed on me in a foolish way the loan of her
> flat in Vienna, which I could not have used, she

expatiated on the good impression I had made
on her at some meeting a few days before, told
me about her affair with the English diplomat,
which I thought was probably untrue, and em-
braced me fervently, flailing her arms about so
that she broke my mother's workbox on the
floor. I was puzzled to know why H. G. had sent
me this peculiar person.

Later on 20 June, a day during which the temper-
ature reached 91 degrees, Wells turned Frau Gatternigg brusquely away. "I was harsh and savage with
her and smashed the door on her too hard so to
speak," he wrote to Rebecca, "but I was tired and
suffering nervously and she was unspeakably tiresome—you cannot imagine how tiresome. A gnawing
incessant little rat she was, threatening all my peace
with you and everything I cared for. Incessantly
begging money and time and attention." [9] That evening Frau Gatternigg attempted to kill herself in
Wells's flat. Wells was absent at the time, and it was
Jane who discovered her at 4 Whitehall Court. Jane
called the police, who saw to it that Frau Gatternigg
was taken to a hospital. The reporters got wind of
the affair, and one of them learned from Frau Gatternigg's landlady of her visit to Rebecca. There-
upon they descended *en masse* on Rebecca, enquiring
about what they called Frau Gatternigg's "scene with
her over H. G." earlier in the day and seeking to
photograph her with Anthony.

The *Star* broke the story the next day. The *New
York Times* provides the following summary of this
article:

WOMAN TRIES SUICIDE
IN FLAT OF H. G. WELLS

Mrs. Guttenig [*sic*], Austrian
Translator of His Works, Cuts Throat
—Likely to Recover—

London. June 22— The Evening Star last night printed an account of an extraordinary incident that occurred Wednesday evening in the flat occupied by H. G. Wells, the novelist, in Whitehall Court, Westminster.

Mr. Wells was dressing for dinner at 7:30 o'clock, when a woman called, asked to see him, and was shown into his study to wait till he had completed his change of costume.

When Mr. Wells entered the study his visitor, who was greatly excited, told him she was going to commit suicide. He tried to calm her and left her sitting in a chair while he went downstairs to request the porter of the flat to communicate with the police.

On his return to his study Mr. Wells was horrified to see his visitor walking around the room with blood flowing from a terrible wound in her throat. It had been inflicted with a razor, which she still held in her right hand.

Mr. Wells at once went toward her but before he could reach her she collapsed on the floor. Assistance was summoned, and it was then discovered that the injured woman was wearing only a nightdress under her long coat. She was removed in an ambulance to a hospital, and it is expected that she will recover.

At the hospital a letter was found in her possession which, according to The Star made
"strange statements."

The Star added that before going to Mr.
Wells' flat, the woman visited the apartments of
a well-known woman novelist in Kensington and
there acted in a strange manner.

Mr. Wells, in conversation with a newspaper
representative, said he did not feel called upon
to make public the details of the occurrence.

"An extraordinary report has gained currency
of something which occurred in a private
house," he said. "Something of the kind did
happen, but the facts as reported are incorrect
and exaggerated. I do not want the thing talked
about, and the less I hear about it the better. I
am not going to add to the snowball at all."

Great reticence concerning the affair was observed by the police and also at the institutions
where the woman was treated. Scotland Yard
refused to make any statement and officials at
both Charing Cross Hospital and Westminster
Infirmary declined to speak about the case. The
woman was first taken to Charing Cross Hospital and then to Westminster Infirmary where
she is still under the care of physicians.[10]

On 23 June a substantial story appeared in the
Daily News, with shorter accounts in the *Daily Herald*
and *Daily Express* and a brief follow-up in the *Star.*
Further journalistic enterprise could have been devastating, since Wells's statement to the papers had
been guarded and misleading. Indeed, there were

Kensington Gardens
Friday June 23.23

Panther supporting the wounded Jaguar, 23 June 1923

innuendoes in the *Star's* initial report that suggested impending revelations. In a state approaching panic, Wells pleaded with Rebecca to stand by him during this critical period, and she did so. He took her ostentatiously to the Ivy Restaurant and the theatre, as if daring acquaintances to inquire about the newspaper reports with which London was buzzing. She suggested that he appeal to the Newspaper Owners' Association through Beaverbrook and Riddell to prevent further notice of the affair. Wells persuaded her to intervene on his behalf instead, saying ("a little too sensibly," Rebecca later noted) that they liked her better than they did him. Rebecca succeeded in her mission, but the situation was still potentially dangerous. Frau Gatternigg remained in London, initially in Westminster Infirmary and then at a nursing home. It was discovered on examination that "her cuts . . . [were] malingerer's cuts—she was in a hospital for three years—and not sincere cuts. No artery was severed." [11] An uncontrollable scandal could have resulted from Frau Gatternigg's death. At the time the questioning of witnesses during an inquest was brutal. Wells would have suffered, but Rebecca's examination on the assumption that she was a depraved woman who had insulted a rival would altogether have ruined her. This was no longer to be feared. Nevertheless, "Lady Astor took up the girl's case and was hovering round the sickbed to take up her crusading weapons." [12] And though the Duchinskys wrote Wells letters of "effusive apology," Frau Gatternigg herself was quite impenitent, deriving great satisfaction indeed from playing her role of "Heroine of Romance." [13] It was some weeks before she could be gotten back once more to Austria. Even then he was not entirely free of her. In a letter to her mother of 24 October he declined to send any further sums for Frau Gatternigg's translation into German of *Men Like Gods,* stating that he had already "paid her over £150 with absolutely nothing in return," and noting that she had done her best "to create an ugly and injurious scandal about me." [14]

This experience confirmed Rebecca's resolution to break finally with Wells. She afterwards noted that

not once did he say "I am sorry I have got you into this." He simply used me for his protection, and had no other thought about me. I felt he was really insane with selfishness, and it was also extremely puzzling why he should have selected this unattractive and obviously eccentric Austrian to have an affair with—and again why when that had happened, he had sent her to me. I was desperately anxious from that moment to get quit of all connection with both H. G. and Jane.

By the end of June, Rebecca felt able to leave for the Hotel Klinger in Marienbad, where doctors hoped that she would recover from the anemia that beset her. Wells pursued her with letters in which he gave her the latest bulletins concerning "the Gatternigg" and reiterated his love for her in what was for him a curiously indirect and timid fashion, as if he were no longer sure of his standing. Cats "turned out to wander in the street" fall into "mischief" and have "unpleasant adventures." [15] Lovers need constant reassurance; otherwise there is the danger of their employing "what might be called an inferior substitute." [16] For ten days Rebecca did not reply. When she finally broke her silence, Wells immediately entered into arrangements for his arrival in Marienbad as Mr. West. Rebecca then objected to the assurance with which he made these proposals and deprecated the sensual tone of his letters, and in his reply Wells amused himself with the pretense that he spoke with two voices, his own and that

Two sketches from a love letter, mid-July 1923

which he used when "the Leo Tolstoi" control was
dominant. He would try to think of walks and literary talk in his best "LT" manner, not of the more
physical things that mattered to "HG." [17]

Rebecca had been quite content at Marienbad, taking the cure with an American friend of long standing, Mrs. Christie Miller, and Reginald Turner's
sister-in-law, Gwladys Lawson. The ladies were "the
pets of their doctor," and they enjoyed the quiet routine that he had established for them. Wells's arrival
changed all this. He was in an unhappy frame of
mind, insisting "that he was ruined, that the whole
world was against him because he stood for peace,"
and spoiling for trouble. He took the ladies to a
nightclub, where there was "a difficult scene" because he refused to buy champagne as custom demanded, and in general he effectively destroyed Rebecca's peace, even alienating her favorite doctor,
who "could not quite take their much advertised relationship." Wells later recognized, as he told Rebecca, that "you were happy at Marienbad until I
came and spoilt it." [18]

CHAPTER XI *The Sword That Severs All*

So the situation continued through the fall of 1923. Wells would not divorce Jane and marry Rebecca, but when she asked him for £3,000 a year instead, well knowing that he would refuse this demand, he countered by giving her $20,000 from his American royalties, and he promised to make provisions for Anthony. They passed some days in September at Eastbourne and Swanage with Anthony and his nurse, and they made occasional automobile excursions together. Otherwise, their meetings were chiefly in public, once at Ciro's, where as Wells aggrievedly put it, "she has her gossips and dancing and a general clatter of suchlike to alleviate me." [1] Charges of frivolity and idleness, it may be mentioned, are henceforth increasingly common in Wells's letters. They had little foundation. Rebecca almost never went dancing, and when she arose late in the morning, it was usually because she had passed the night in writing. His complaints really stemmed from the inevitable divergence in friends

and interests resulting from their twenty-six years'
difference in age. But Wells would not admit this to
himself, and he dotted his letters with protests
against what he saw as Rebecca's cavalier treatment
of him:

Poor Jaguar!
Alone
in London.
His Panther
taking it Easy
in the Paysage.
What will happen to him?
Exposed to
Dangers!
Temptations!
Hoories?
Glad Eyes!
and him so weak.
Possibly he is frown over altogether
If not
will she receive him
and love him
as ever.

Bored. Wants his Black Pussy. His *dear* Black
Pussy. His soft *kind* Pussy. His *only* Pussy—all
others being shams and mutations. Wants to
know when she is coming back to him. Nobody
licks his fur properly 'cept Her. Nobody yowls
back same as she does. Wants to take Handsful
of her dear soft hair and stroke her Magnificent
Flanks and ——. Ssh! [2]

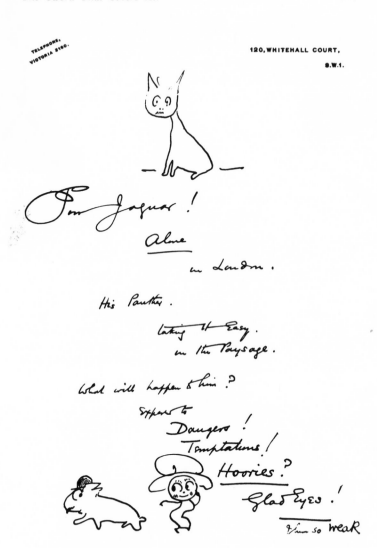

Jaguar alone and exposed to temptation, 1923

On 20 October Rebecca set off on her long-deferred American tour with the fixed intention of making this enforced separation the means of ensuring the termination of her ten-year relationship with Wells. He pursued her with whimsical cards on which desolate cats kept count of the days by which "the Great Silence" was extending itself and suggested that there was always the possibility of "a Ginger Pussy and Consolation." [3] Rebecca's first letter left Wells dissatisfied, when it at last arrived on 14 November. Sensing that their final break was impending, he perhaps found it a matter of pride to propose the severance himself:

> She didn't write for a week. She was just old enjoying herself. She wasn't in trouble. She didn't want help. She just gadded. Shall I chuck her *now?* I am getting used to her not being about and she is getting used to my not being about. Go my own way and let her go hers? She's young, excitable, wilful, voracious and as a matter of fact she goes her own way now. [4]

15. XI. 23

Jaguar receives Panther's first letter from the United States, 15 November 1923

Four days later he enlarged on his discontents:

> If there is any prospect of your prolonging
> your American tour or of getting on to see the
> Cañons of Colorado or San Francisco or the
> South Seas I think you had better take it. My
> health seems to be in a very much worse way than
> I thought and I don't think there's anything
> here in England for you to come home to. . . .
> If I'm to get straight again I must lead a vale-
> tudinarian life for a time in some warm climate.
> Now you with your lively and impatient charac-
> ter aren't going to be any good to me in that
> state. You would be bored to death and you
> would bore me from the time when you didn't
> get up in the morning to the time when you
> didn't come home from the Hotel Dance at
> night. I don't even want to try the experiment.
> You and I have always been such good com-
> panions that I don't see why we shouldn't be
> frank about all this. You are much too alive and
> much too discursively jolly to stand being teth-
> ered to me any longer and I'm far too concen-
> trated upon what is myself to stand any more of
> your bright irrelevant activities. The Cats must
> follow their Destinies and their Destinies di-
> verge. No reason why they shouldn't be still two
> very loving Cats—with all the world between
> them.[5]

Wells found it a particular grievance that Rebecca
had not been candid with him, evolving an imaginary conspiracy out of his brooding:

The promised second letter doesn't come.—I doubt it ever will. The Lynds have been here and Sylvia talked about our situation. She knew all about it. I didn't understand before how carefully you Radcliffe and Letty and the Friends generally had planned this American breach and it seems to me a little bit mean that you couldn't have been open with me and broken decently and friendly last spring. . . .

Now that the Great Silence has done its job I'd like to know at times how you are getting on. I don't like asking people like Radcliffe and Sylvia for the news of you.[6]

When he did hear again from Rebecca, he took particular umbrage at her brevity and restraint. His pain and resentment found various outlets. He would create a life for himself without her.

I warned you this spring that to keep a love alive and going a certain amount of attention is needed. Mine doesn't get it and it's practically dead. You're a great dear and a wonderful person but I don't look forward with any excitement to meeting you again. I was bored to death by all that foolery at Marienbad and bored in London. I mean to create a new atmosphere for myself in Portugal without you. I now know that you've been planning for a year to get along without me. You do get along without me and there you are! Why not face the facts? [7]

He satirically envisioned Rebecca beating Hugh Walpole at his own game and becoming "our star interpreter" in the United States. He derided Rebecca's further allusions to her desire for marriage.

> I don't see why you should always tuck in your sense of humour when you are dealing with me and why Jane should be dragged in forever in our little differences. You would have gone to California if we had been ten times married and you would have jazzed, bored me with your [Michael] Arlen and [Stacey] Aumonier and such like and done everything you suddenly wanted to do just as you do now. Why humbug about it? And unless you really think that I was prepared to trail after your lecturing tour like an American husband, what difference would marriage make to our present situation?

He threatened to take Anthony away from her:

> I'm inclined to think I ought to adopt him. A boy ought to have a man in his life. I've told Gyp about him and I shall tell Frank when a favourable occasion arises and I think they'll be good elders for him.[8]

Yet in all these letters there are reminders of Wells's profound longing and affection for Rebecca.

In early January of 1924 Wells left for the Hotel Miramar at Mont'Estoril near Lisbon, where he was soon joined by his secretary and the doctor husband she had just acquired. His health improved in this warm, quiet setting, "a sort of Algeciras with a much better hinterland." [9] No doubt it couldn't compare with "the Rockies and San Francisco," but it was "amoosing in detail and the strata of humanity are

deeper and older." [10] The Galsworthys introduced
him everywhere, and he spent his time working,
walking, and playing tennis and roulette. The young
red-haired widow of an army officer provided consolation of another sort. His letters to Rebecca became
dry, laconic, and precisely phrased, as if he were
played out after the alarms and excursions of the
preceding year. Indeed, Anthony was the only topic
that stirred him to much animation: "Our Son is one
of the dearest little beasts in the world. We mixed
very well then whatever we have done since." [11] Elsewhere he compared his life in Portugal with that he
presumed Rebecca to be living in the United States.

> Flowers, sunshine, long walks, picnics among
> the rocks, storms, green waves, foam mountains
> high; the simple innocent life the Jaguar loves.
> Compare Panther rolling in bootleggers, Bea-
> verbrooks and coloured people, studying the
> drug traffic and generally going it. A Black Pan-
> ther. A white Jaguar with blue eyes. The Bride
> of Pleasure and the Bride of Prayer.[12]

When Rebecca received this letter she must have
been struck by the ironic contrast between Wells's
description of her as a "Bride of Pleasure" and the
shape her life had actually taken in the United
States. She had seen her long-deferred American
trip as a decisive hazard of new fortunes. Not only
was it to confirm her break with Wells, it was also to
bring order to her existence in other ways. Her position in England remained highly speculative. During
her ten years with Wells her life had been too agi-
tated and distracting to permit her to accept a staff

job on a newspaper or indeed to be sure of fulfilling
any commission. Her mother had died in 1920. She
had many acquaintances but few friends. Hence she
thought for a time that, if she could establish herself
as a writer in New York, perhaps writing features
for a magazine or a newspaper, she might make a
home there for Anthony. At first, this goal seemed
within her grasp.

She took to the United States. In Philadelphia her
reception was kind, and people liked what she had to
say. She had been taught by her father to lecture
without notes in the manner of most good English
speakers. Her facility impressed sophisticated east-
ern audiences, but further west this way of doing
things was sometimes interpreted as implying a lack
of proper preparation. As she proceeded to Chicago,
Minneapolis, Indianapolis, St. Louis, Rockford (Illinois), and Iowa City, her reception continued to be
favorable, but she came to feel that this sort of work
was hardly at her level. When she returned to Chicago, she was nonetheless still in lively spirits. She
wrote to S. K. Ratcliffe:

> I find it very difficult to foresee my audiences
> from their titles. The Women's Athletic Club of
> Chicago I had imagined to be a collection of
> husky young women in sweaters. They turned
> out to be a collection of elderly ladies who cer-
> tainly weighed 250 lbs apiece and wore all the
> Crown jewels. They explained their title by say-
> ing that they had a swimming tank in the base-
> ment. I could hardly refrain from asking what
> on earth happened if two of them got in at once.

> They were a little difficult to instruct on the sub-
> ject of the Spirit and Tendency of the Modern
> Novel, and I left out the passage dealing with
> the defects of James Joyce's aesthetic theory—
> but they seemed to enjoy it.[13]

When the Omaha papers called her lecture in-
comprehensible and her delivery halting, defects
which had passed unnoticed in other cities, she
asked herself if it were not too much trouble to
gauge such a market.

It was with relief that Rebecca returned to New
York for Christmas. There she encountered another
complication. Before her departure from England, a
couple she had known well for years reached an ami-
cable parting of the ways. The wife called on Rebecca to tell her the news and startled her by suddenly saying that of course Rebecca must have
known that her husband was in love with her and
would certainly ask her to marry him when the final
arrangements for separation were completed. During her lecture tour Rebecca received kind and soli-
citous letters from him, and on reaching New York
she found him waiting for her. They were happy
together for two weeks, and then there was a tragic
interruption, which meant that he returned to England, though they were still in love, and for some
years afterwards he made agonizing reappearances
in her life.

On the rebound from this affair Rebecca fell ill
with influenza, which left her with bronchitis and
colitis. The remainder of her lecture tour was post-
poned for two months while she made her way back

to health. She was particularly grateful for the friendships that she formed:

> The novelist Fannie Hurst was an angel to me. She was the only person who saw that I was ill and tired and unhappy to a dangerous degree. Her patience with me and her generosity are things marvellous to recall. I also got to know Alec Woollcott, who was too egoistic to notice what was happening to me, but who poured out bounty on me because he approved of me. Carl van Vechten, and his wife Fania Marinoff, Franklin P. Adams the columnist, Bruce and Beatrice Gould of the Ladies Home Journal, Arthur and Martha Krock, they all devoted themselves to giving me a good time. I had already known for some time Doris Stevens, the feminist, and the curious disreputable and grandiose lawyer to whom she was then married, Dudley Field Malone, and they were protective angels. I formed a special and immediate friendship with Emanie Sachs, the wife of Walter Sachs, who, still, now Emanie Phillips, wife of August Phillips, is my friend. She was, like me, something of an odd man out. She wrote brilliantly, but writers distrusted her as a member of the bourgeoisie and the bourgeoisie distrusted her because she was a brilliant writer.

Yet despite the attentions of these new friends, this was an uneasy time for Rebecca. She quickly discovered that her status in New York was ambiguous, that she was regarded as an outsider, even as a freak. Her separation from Wells being common gossip,

her new acquaintances assumed that he had provided her with a substantial income. In the midst of
a party Ruth Hale, the wife of Heywood Broun,
stood up and, catching the ears of the entire company, said:

> Rebecca West, we are all disappointed in you.
> You have put an end to a great illusion. We
> thought of you as an independent woman, but
> here you are, looking down in the mouth, be-
> cause you relied on a man to give you all you
> wanted and now that you have to turn out and
> fend for yourself you are bellyaching about it. I
> believe Wells treated you too darn well, he gave
> you money and jewels and everything you
> wanted and if you live with a man on those
> terms you must expect to get turned out when
> he gets tired of you.

The drawing room quickly emptied itself during this
remarkable speech, but to Rebecca's astonishment
the host and hostess made no apologies, and the incident was treated as a comic interlude which she
ought to take in good part. Rebecca did not see why.
Hardly more agreeable was the occasion on which
the Scott Fitzgeralds gave a party for her. Fitzgerald
forgot his promise to fetch her, and she accordingly
spent the evening in her hotel room, dressed for the
party and ringing up friends in an unsuccessful attempt to discover where he lived, while Fitzgerald
did an imitation of her for his amused guests. Her
supposed rudeness became the talk of the town.
Again, she was commissioned by a newspaper to
write an account of a famous charity ball. The staff

member that the newspaper had sent to accompany
her became noisy and drunk, and Rebecca in desper-
ation left early with friends, her writing chore un-
done. Her escort sought to cover his tracks by asserting that Miss West had become so drunk that he had
had to take her home. Rebecca's friends put the
record straight, but the story did her no good. Rebecca grew terrified of what the clubwomen who had
once called for her deportation might do with such
episodes as these. By the end of her stay in New
York she was seeing only Fannie Hurst, Doris Ste-
vens, and the Roumanian short-story writer Konrad
Bercovici, whom she found particularly kindly and
large-hearted.

Rebecca had finally to admit that her dream of
making a new life for herself and Anthony in the
United States was not destined to be realized. It
seemed for a time, indeed, that she would not even
succeed in climbing the slippery slopes of American
journalism. There were many offers of employment,
but few that stood up to close scrutiny. At the last
moment, however, Irita Van Doren, acting for the
owners of the *Herald Tribune,* who had heard from
Alexander Woollcott of her humiliations and embar-
rassments, offered Rebecca a position. She was to
come to America for two months each year, in the
spring and in the fall, as a contributor to the literary
section of that paper. All her expenses were to be
paid and a liberal fee provided.

In March she resumed her lecture tour, which car-
ried her as far as the west coast before she returned
to England in May. America, for all its trials, had
done her good. She was immensely refreshed, she

was swimming once more in the currents of general life, and she had an anchor for her professional future.

In early June Rebecca and Wells encountered each other by chance in a London theatre. "Meeting you has left me sick and sorrowful with love for you," he wrote to her the next day. "Never mind about it dear, but I want you to know." [14] In another note he continued:

> I won't ring you up on Thursday unless you do me. I don't want to crowd you up. I've had a wave of *feeling* about you and perhaps it had better cool off. You are the woman of my life and I've got a great desire to liquidate what is left of our old bankruptcy and get back to terms again. In your own time. . . .
>
> I love you very much and I don't want to hamper or distress you any more.[15]

And later in the months he added: "I have had a day of longing for you and I know I shall be your lover to the day of my death." [16] This gentle mood did not last through the summer. By August he was writing in the old vein.

> Dear Sweet Phantom Panther.
>
> I've always been in love with you and I always shall be. I saw you just at the last and I think you saw your Phantom Jaguar—too late. Maybe we shall never see each other again. That damned Rebecca West is taking you off to lose you in Austria and H. G. will float about in Lon-

don and go to Geneva and then he will try to
find a place to live in through the winters in the
south of France or Corsica or Algiers with some
sort of body slave. And I don't care how soon
the whole show ends. Cicely Fairfield is just a
Fairfield and Rebecca is a wilful impulsive bitch
and Panther (damn the Holdsworths for calling
you Panther!) Panther is my lost love and a
black hole in my heart.

Jaguar [17]

For a time, indeed, Wells was haunted by Rebecca.
His feeling for her reached a pitch comparable to
that which he had experienced at the beginning of
their relationship. He proposed by telegram to her
in Austria that they spend the winter with Anthony
in Montpellier, an invitation which she refused without a qualm. She was determined not to jeopardize
the order that her separation from him had enabled
her to bring into her life. Moreover, she had heard
from common friends that Wells was putting it about
that he had in fact left her because of her laziness
and extravagance, a canard that greatly offended
her. In his irritation Wells threatened to stop seeing
Anthony: "You've taken yourself away from me and
you'd better take him too. Disagreeable? Well, I
loved you pretty badly." [18] But his "cross letter" was
followed immediately by a note of apology.[19]

As Wells began to admit to himself that this time
Rebecca was not coming back, appeals for reconciliation were replaced in his letters by references to the
"new and stupendous book" that he was writing.

I want to see you and tell you about the *Form* of my book. It's a new releasing sort of Form that leaves your hands free for quite beautiful writing. . . .

You and I have an excess of wit and brain and interest. The well constructed novel is an intolerable servitude for us. The story ought to be implicit and not categorically told.[20]

This remarkable work was *The World of William Clissold,* which may usefully be examined in conjunction with another book by Wells, *The Research Magnificent* of 1915, since both contain characters that were suggested in part by Rebecca. Each novel recounts the career of a thoughtful man of affairs, who makes his mark in practical life, but at the same time sees as his real commitment "the peace of the world-state, the open conspiracy of all the sane men in the world against the things that break us up into wars and futilities."[21] Women are important both to Benham, the hero of Wells's earlier book, and to Clissold, but less important ultimately than doing the work that is their destiny.

Amanda in *The Research Magnificent,* which was written in 1913–1914, is Rebecca as Wells first knew her, an eager, forthright, impulsive girl of nineteen. Benham finds her "the freest, finest, bravest spirit that he had ever encountered." For a while their love affair is an adventure lived by "Leopard" and "Cheetah"—two of the "great carnivora"—defying the world from their "lair." They experience "Heroic Love to its highest note." Yet their harmony is not perfect. Amanda has a will of her own that she means to impose whether or not Benham agrees, and the "stark frankness" that had so attracted him to her turns out to be compatible with an ability to act an "intricate part" in a drama of deception. Moreover, there is a "basic conflict of intellectual temperaments" between them. At the beginning her very vigor enchants him:

> there was something delightful in her pounce, even when she was pouncing on things superficial, vulgar or destructive. She made him understand and share the excitement of a big night at the opera, the glitter and prettiness of a smart restaurant, the clustering little acute adventures of a great reception of gay people, . . . She picked up the art world where he had laid it down, and she forced him to feel dense and slow before he rebelled against her multitudinous enthusiasms and admiration.

But at last Benham comes to see Amanda as "an animated discursiveness," absorbed in "the dramatic side of life," who can never understand his need for intellectual order and purpose. Though their child keeps them together for a time, they finally "drift into antagonism and estrangement," Amanda is attracted to another man, and they part.[22]

When Wells devised this conclusion for Amanda's story, he was yielding to the necessity of demonstrating Benham's exclusive devotion to the "Research Magnificent," rather than prophesying how his relationship with Rebecca would end. The much briefer study of Helen in *The World of William Clissold,* which Wells wrote at Lou Bastidon in 1924 and

1925, embodies his reflections on the way the end actually came about nearly ten years later.[23] It deserves close examination for its record of how Wells had come to regard his years with Rebecca, or at any rate of how he wanted to persuade himself that he had come to regard them. Significantly, he now puts Rebecca actually on the stage:

> Only the reader who was in love with Helen could see her as I saw her. For other people she was a strong, clever, ambitious actress with a charming smile, an adorable voice, a reputation for a hot temper, and an ungracious way with obtrusive admirers. Many people found her beautiful, but no one called her pretty. She was a mistress to be proud of, but only a brave man would attempt to steal her.[24]

This was what had become, he is asserting, of the passionate free spirit of nineteen he had met so long ago.

Their early years together, in which they lived "romantically, ostentatiously" as "lovers, friends, allies and companions" are passed over in a paragraph, but it is in this context that Wells tries to define the special quality by which Rebecca held him:

> What a lovely thing Helen was—and is! She not only evoked and satisfied my sense of beauty in herself, but she had the faculty of creating a kind of victorious beauty in the scene about her. She had a vision that transformed things, annexed them, and made them tributary to her magic ensemble.[25]

Then Wells comes to his real subject: why they quarrelled and parted. He did not respect her work, nor did she respect his, and their relationship interfered with the things they wanted to do.

> We could feel together, but we could make no sacrifice for our feelings. Ours was an intensely sympathetic and an intensely selfish fellowship. . . . It was from my side that the first revelation of dissevering motives came. But when I had been with her a little time, and when I was fully assured of her, then aglow with happiness and fit and energetic, I would hear the call of my business operations and of my political interests as a call to self-completion. All the other women I had ever had to deal with since I became an actively prosperous man had accepted these inattentions and disappearances as things in the course of nature. I had been used to go away to my real life. But my going away, becoming customary, must have impressed Helen as the supreme outrage. Because, you see, it was not that I went away to see to tiresome, necessary things; that might have been forgiven. But I went away to things because they were more important to me. She was incidental and they were essential! It was incredible.[26]

But if Clissold had thus taken the initiative, he admits that it did not remain with him long. "At first I was stronger than Helen, and I was overbearing with her and thoughtless and cruel. But she was younger than I was and with greater powers of variation and recuperation, and a time soon came when she was stronger than I." [27] When Wells depicts Helen's social circle in passing, he is no doubt also recording his view of Rebecca's "little friends":

> I found it saturated with an excessive self-consciousness, with a craving for strong unsound effects; its lack of intellectual conscience continually amazed me. It was pervaded by sly and hovering young men and by habitually self-explanatory women who made up their personalities as they made up their faces. It never seemed sure whether it was smart or Bohemian. It affected a sort of universal friendship and great liberties of endearment. It sat about at unusual hours and gossipped and talked about itself, endlessly, emptily. And collectively it was up to nothing at all.[28]

The end came when marriage was put forward as a step that would somehow make everything different.

> It was only too plain to me that nothing would be different. We parted again with some heat and bitterness and had a second inconclusive reconciliation. I had never before begged for mercy from a woman, but I confess I did from her. What did I beg of her? That she would be in some profound and fundamental way different, that she should not be herself in fact, in order that I should be myself. What did I really want of her?
>
> There were times when I behaved like a thwarted child. She had become a habit of mind with me. I beat myself against her. I stopped thinking about things in general. I neglected

business. She had got my imagination so entangled with her that for a while it would not serve me for any end of my own. I came near to a complete surrender and to giving her a marriage that would have done nothing at all for either of us. And then, filled with wrath, not so much with her as with myself, I set myself, sullenly and steadily, to break those humiliating and intolerable bonds.

I told her that now at last we had come to the end of our relationship.

We parted in a phase of grim anger—and she started out upon the subjugation of South Africa.

How completely had this hard, ambitious young woman changed from the dark, tall girl I had loved! And how swiftly so soon as she departed did she become again the dark, tall girl I had found so splendidly lovable! How I longed to hear her voice once more and see her again with my eyes! Directly she had gone I was asking myself why I had let her go. I forgot that for three years she had been going away from me far more than I had been going away from her, and it seemed to me simply that I had let her go. The love alone was remembered; the quarrels all forgotten. Why had I let her go?

And at the same time, cold and clear in me disregardful of my general tumult and dominant over all, was my decision that we had to part.[29]

Wells admits that it would take "the intricate faithfulness of a Henry James" to convey the "comings and goings, moods hidden and betrayed, insensible changes of attitude" that actually belonged to the story he was telling.[30] But when he presents his surrogate, Clissold, as a sage of broad vision, who despite his endearing human foibles is able to rise above the distractions offered by his dazzling but superficial mistress and firmly direct their joint course towards a painful but necessary separation, one wonders at his capacity for self-deception.

CHAPTER XII *Aftermath*

"The union of this ever-diverse pair" has now been described, but the story of Wells and Rebecca would be incomplete without some account of their life apart from each other during the years which followed their separation. From 1924 to 1927 "things went along fairly indifferently" between them.[1] Wells's routine remained much as it had been, except that Odette Keun took Rebecca's place in his life. Because Wells needed sunshine, this new pair fell into the habit of wintering near Grasse in Provence, first at Lou Bastidon, a simple house among olive trees, and later at Lou Pidou, the more elaborate home which they built for themselves. If Wells saw Rebecca infrequently, their relations were at least not acutely uncomfortable. As already noted, he had given her £5,000, in part as a repayment of legacies from her mother and grandmother which had been used for their common expenses, and he usually paid Anthony's school bills of £80 a term.

Their chief remaining bond was Anthony. At

Wells's suggestion he had been placed in 1924 at St. Piran's, Maidenhead. Major Bryant, Wells's friend and disciple from Oundle, was headmaster at St. Piran's, and Wells was persuaded that the boy would "find a hovering Providence" there "to ease his distresses." [2] Wells visited Anthony's school from time to time while Rebecca was in America. On one of these occasions, indeed, he incautiously "paraded his parenthood before the other children so that some of them tormented the child about it." [3] But after it became evident to Wells that Rebecca was not going to return to him, his attentions to Anthony fell off. "I don't think there's much use my going on seeing the small boy," he told her, "if that's all you want to see me for." [4] He protested when Anthony expressed a desire to become a Roman Catholic, a development in which he saw the malign influence of Letty, but otherwise he was disposed to withdraw more and more from his son's life. He had told Rebecca in October 1924:

> I don't know what to do about Anthony. I hate the Westminster tradition about as much as I hate the Roman Catholic stunt but I feel I can't pull the poor little devil about. You've got him on your hands. I'm not likely to see very much of you from now on and I don't see how we can hope to cooperate in so subtle and complicated a matter as his up-bringing. And what is the good of my writing letters to him? What is there to write about now? We've broken. Am I to tell him that? He's not going to see me again for years.[5]

The middle 1920s were a difficult time for Rebecca. Though her reputation as a writer grew steadily, her financial arrangements remained precarious. She had only her fees from the *Herald Tribune,* her £ 300 a year of interest on Wells's gift, and the few journalistic commissions that she had the time and energy to fulfill among the many that were offered to her. Hard-pressed to make ends meet, she had to worry constantly about unpaid bills. If she was nonetheless able to maintain a comfortable home in London and even to manage vacations in the south of France for herself and Anthony, this feat was accomplished by the narrowest of margins. Moreover, her position in society remained uncomfortable. The hostility of Jane's friends had not diminished. She was haunted, for example, by the insolence that Arnold Bennett had shown to her throughout a dinner given by A. P. Herbert. She was not asked to the sports days and prize givings at Anthony's schools until he was admitted to Stowe. Even at that model institution, where Dr. Roxburgh, the headmaster, was "a paragon of enlightenment," no master spoke to her on these occasions, though one of them, who had acted as a tutor to Anthony in the south of France (" £ 5 a week and the Mediterranean in the back garden") used to show her "surreptitious kindnesses" on her other visits to the school. It was small consolation to reflect that this neglect did not stem from malice, that it was simply thought best not to draw attention to her. Rebecca and the man from whom she had parted in New York continued to be in love, but their brief reunions every six months or so were unsettling rather than satisfying. She told

Wells nothing of this affair, leaving him to believe instead that she had a variety of suitors, as was indeed the case. "I had your letter detailing your shocking treatment of your Aspirants," he wrote to her on one occasion. "Some day a man will kill you, not for love but just out of annoyance. And then you will be sorry." [6] She could understand Wells's bewilderment during their rare meetings when he found her disturbed and sad yet unwilling to consider returning to him.

Meanwhile, there was trouble at St. Piran's. Anthony had complained about the school from the first, and though Rebecca was not impressed by the evidence which he adduced, her visits there did persuade her that its atmosphere was decidedly odd. Finally Major Bryant was arrested for drunken driving, and it came to light that his wife, a victim like Rebecca's mother of exophthalmic goiter, had for some time been pushing him towards a breakdown by her eccentric behavior. With Wells's concurrence, given after an inquiry as to whether "the Bryant trouble is, so to speak, conclusive," [7] Rebecca removed Anthony from St. Piran's and placed him at a preparatory school in Hampstead, where the headmaster, Mr. Wathen, proved kind and sympathetic. It was intended that after a year there he should be entered in a public school, preferably Stowe.

In May of 1927 Jane learned that she had terminal cancer. This discovery was a shock for which both she and Wells were altogether unprepared. He set out from Provence to be with her in London during her few remaining months. When Rebecca wrote to him, she received only a short note in reply: "I've

had a strange time for the last five months and I'm
more tired and depleted than ever I have been. I'll
not forget you're there. We must have a talk one
day." [8] They met after Jane's death on 6 October,
and before Wells returned to Provence he put his solicitors, Messrs. Gedge, Fiske, and Gedge, to work on
arrangements for Anthony's financial future. It took
some time to resolve this matter, but thanks largely
to Odette's continued pressure relatively modest re-
vocable trusts were eventually settled on the boy. He
was to receive the income from one of these at the
age of eighteen, from the other at twenty, and the
capital at thirty. There was no provision for Rebecca.
"You may marry again," Wells told her, "or bring off
a big success before then." [9] The "again" in this sentence offers a significant clue to Wells's way of
regarding his relationship with Rebecca.

Even before he came to England, Wells had asked
Anthony to arrange to meet Gip. Nothing having
come of this approach, Wells returned to the subject
in a letter to Rebecca just before he went back to
Provence:

> Would you write to Gip and arrange a meeting?
> A big Half Brother might be rather a nice nov-
> elty for Anthony. They both draw and they both
> have a zoological disposition. I'd see to this my-
> self but I'm going off and I didn't know how
> Gip felt in the matter. I never like to force peo-
> ple together, but yesterday the suggestion came
> from him. [10]

Anthony did become friends with Gip and Frank,
but his first visit to Easton Glebe at Christmas of

1927 was the cause of much recrimination. Rebecca
was annoyed at having her holiday plans upset by
Wells's belated invitation, and Wells complained
about confusion in the arrangements for Anthony's
visit. Wells wrote: "Evidently it is no longer possible
for us to correspond. . . . I see no advantage and
every possibility of friction in dealing with or about
him through you." [11] To which Rebecca replied: "I
think your suggestion that we should not communicate directly about Anthony excellent. . . .
This will be my last letter to you." [12] Though this
little storm soon blew itself out, in its wake Wells and
Rebecca exhibited a certain wariness to each other.
When Rebecca wrote cordially of Odette Keun,
whom she had come to know and like, Wells replied:

> There is no need to tell me to be good to Odette
> because I am good to everybody. It is my way.
> She will write to you in a few days time. She says
> you have got my psychology wrong, but in these
> Questions of Specialists I cannot interfere.[13]

When Rebecca and Anthony returned from their
Easter holiday in 1928 it was discovered that the boy
was gravely ill. His trouble was diagnosed as tuberculosis by a specialist who recommended a sanatorium
near Holt in Norfolk. Rebecca took him down by
car, a long journey which she afterwards discovered
might have been fatal to him since it turned out that
he was actually suffering from an uncommon type of
pneumonia then causing a number of deaths among
what the medical journals called "well-nourished
children." Having installed Anthony in the sanatorium, Rebecca returned to London to put her flat in

order and give notice to her several employers that she would be unable to work. There she herself fell ill of influenza, which for a time left her quite deaf.[14] Having heard of these catastrophes, Wells wrote to her during her convalescence:

> I'm so sorry about you and the cub. It was so jolly to see you well established in your pleasant flat and writing well and prosperous. I smiled and went away. But this misfortune of yours reopens all sorts of shut-down tendernesses and I feel like your dear brother and your best friend and your father and your once (and not quite forgetting it) lover. Count on me for any help you need. I'm still very hopeful about the case, for what comes suddenly may go as suddenly. It is just possible that the cub inherits enough originality to put a sober science like medicine in the wrong.[15]

Wells wrote to Anthony and promised to motor down to see him. This renewed friendliness persisted through June, when Wells attended the first night of a play based on one of Rebecca's stories and told her that "it really made my heart glad to see you having that blaze of success." [16]

After a fortnight of illness, Rebecca returned to Holt. She always remembered with gratitude how John Gunther, in London for a flying visit from Paris where he was stationed as a correspondent, accompanied her to the station and then, seeing how tired and helpless she was, jumped into the train and took her down himself, though he had to go straight back to London. Rebecca was told that Anthony must remain in the sanatorium through the summer and that he ought then to be taken to live in some warm, dry climate such as that offered by South Africa or New Mexico. She did not believe that his condition was so grave, nor did Wells on the one visit which he paid Anthony, but nonetheless for three months she hardly dared leave her Holt hotel. Almost the only redeeming feature of this black experience was that it gave her the courage to break finally with the lover whose intermittent appearances had been disturbing her for four years. Their meeting was painful, and his distracted and resentful reaction left Rebecca grief-stricken, but at least the separation had been accomplished. Finally the doctor in charge of the sanatorium, alerted by the fact that Anthony had inexplicably been putting on weight and gaining strength, recognized that he had never had tuberculosis. Rebecca then consulted another specialist, the ranking authority of the day, who also could find no signs of present or past tuberculosis. From the case history he was of the opinion that the boy had been the victim of the peculiar type of pneumonia already mentioned. He believed that Anthony henceforth would lead a normal life. Following a few more weeks of convalescence, Anthony returned to school, and Rebecca after six lost months was able to resume normal life in London.

Meanwhile, Rebecca's volume of critical essays, *The Strange Necessity,* had appeared in July. As Wells read it, the "tendernesses" which Rebecca's misfortunes had released were once more shut down. In this book she treated Wells's work with a freedom that she had not previously allowed herself. Most of the volume is devoted to a study of Joyce and Proust, but there is also a ground-clearing essay entitled "Uncle Bennett," in which she briefly considered each of the other literary "uncles" of her generation—Galsworthy, Shaw, and Wells—before proceeding to her proper subject:

> Uncle Wells arrived always a little out of breath, with his arms full of parcels, sometimes rather carelessly tied, but always bursting with all manner of attractive gifts that ranged from the little pot of sweet jelly that is "Mr. Polly," to the complete meccano set for the mind that is in The First Men in the Moon. And he brought all the scientific fantasies, and the magic crystals like *Tono-Bungay* and *The New Machiavelli*, in which one could see the forces of the age sweep and surge like smoke about brightly coloured figures that were blinded by them, that saw through them, that were a part of them, that were separate from them and were their enemies, that were separate from them and were their allies, and illustrated as well as it has ever been done the relationship between man and his times.
>
> This impression of wild and surpassing generosity was not in the least one of youth's illusions. One had, in actual fact, the luck to be young just as the most bubbling creative mind that the sun and moon have shone upon since the days of Leonardo da Vinci was showing its form. The only thing against Uncle Wells was that he did so love to shut himself up in the drawing-room and put out all the lights except the lamp with the

pink silk shade, and sit down at the piano and
have a lovely time warbling in too fruity a tenor,
to the accompaniment of chords struck drag-
gingly with the soft pedal held down, songs of
equal merit to "The Rosary."

You know perfectly well what I mean: the
passages where his prose suddenly loses its
firmness and begins to shake like blanc-mange.
"It was then I met Queenie. She was a soft white
slip of being, with very still dark eyes, and a
quality of . . . Furtive scufflings . . . Waste . . .
Modern civilization . . . Waste . . . Parasitic,
greedy speculators. . . . 'Oh, my dear,' she said,
'my dear . . . darn your socks . . . squaw.
. . .' " But take him all in all, Uncle Wells was as
magnificent an uncle as one could hope to
have.[17]

Rebecca's tribute to Wells's achievements is handsome indeed, but he may have been irked at his off-
hand dismissal (two pages, to nearly two hundred
for Joyce and Proust), and certainly her analysis of
his sentimental indulgences and her parody of his
prose touched a nerve. A lively correspondence ensued. Since Rebecca undoubtedly gave as good as
she got, it is particularly to be regretted that her
ripostes can only be dimly inferred:

The *Strange Necessity* is marvellous. It ought to
have music by Stravinsky. And after it is over
the curtain goes up again to reveal Van Loon as
one of the Great Annuals of Literature and you
in your ancient rôle of the Pert but Charming
Niece. I sejuiced you long ago to stop your re-

peating that invention Craye sowed, you watered, and Squire spread about—about Queenie and the Blanc-mange. I can't do it again. You win—so far as you are read.[18]

I didn't *dislike The Strange Necessity.* I only said it ought to have music by Stravinsky. Can't I tickle you in the ribs when you dig into mine? And good critics Pussy, when they want to show a novelist writes about mawkish love affairs, don't just *invent* a silly name for a heroine and silly things she is supposed to say. They quote. But lazy Panthers just repeat their cherished delusions. There never was a Queenie but you've said it so often you've got to believe it.

Don't get bothered about it anyhow—I mean about *The Strange Necessity.* I think you are making your stormy way in it to a critical conclusion. What is the good of an argument between a scalpel and a thunderstorm? [19]

You will have seen how Lynd deals with your book in the *Daily News.* The great critical discoveries give him a headache and he leaves them alone, but how eagerly he jumps on the Queenie lie and quotes every little bit. It is what he has always wanted to believe about my work and here it is said for him by you—who *must* know all about me. All the dears will quote it and quote about the "succulent style"—and after all *your* guidance ought to be final. And the thing is a lie and a damned stupid one. You can go through all my books and list the women characters, not a bad lot from Aunt Ponderevo to Joan

and from Ann Pornick to the "Meanwhile"
women—and you can't find three pages to jus-
tify this spiteful rubbish. It does me no end of
harm; it sets people who haven't read me
against my books; it will be quoted by all the
Lynds in the world. And God knows how you
benefit! [20]

I don't object to criticism but I do object to
slighting and slovenly criticism in what you tell
me is a Critical Essay of quite primary importance. Then the red shades and the throaty
tones become damn silly. If the passage was "almost word for word lifted" from the *Passionate
Friends,* why wasn't it lifted outright in quotes
and why didn't you explain that Rachel is about
as important among my women figures as a traf-
fic policeman in a motor car fire. What's the
good of going off at a tangent from this and
talking about my "confused irritations". It's a
perfectly straight objection to a piece of bad criticism and it's a pity you can't take it in a proper
spirit instead of inventing some complex explanation about a "cranky exile" and so forth, when
you ought to realize that you have had your
little seat spanked in a salutary and entirely private manner.

Well, let that rest. *The Strange Necessity* only
does for your critical side what the *Judge* did for
your pretensions as a novelist. You have a most
elaborate, intricate and elusive style which is ad-
mirably adapted for a personal humorous novel.
It can convey the finest shades of sympathy, rid-

icule and laughter. It is no good whatever for a philosophical discourse any more than it was for a great romance about the tragedy and injustice of life. You are ambitious and pretentious and you do not know the quality and measure of your powers. Some of the *Return of the Soldier* though the style is Conrad-haunted is admirable. Chunks of the *Judge* are magnificent. As a whole it is a sham. It is a beautiful voice and a keen and sensitive mind doing "Big Thinks" to the utmost of its ability—which is nil. God gave you all the gifts needed for a fine and precious artist and he left out humility. And humility in the artist is what charity is in the saint.

There my dear Pussy is some more stuff for your little behind. You sit down on it and think.[21]

Don't be so damned silly. I have never criticized any of your work to anyone except you, save to praise it and advance your interests. Whenever newspaper syndicates have approached me I have invariably told them that you were the goods and so forth and not an old dog like myself. I sent as many people as I could to the *Return of the Soldier*. . . . I refrained from telling even you what I thought of the *Strange Necessity* until your silliness provoked me. And there for me the matter ends.[22]

Determined on reprisal against Rebecca, Wells saw Anthony as the instrument readiest to his hand. "Anthony is going to be a very charming and worthwhile young man," Wells told her, "and it will be a

pity if his prospects are injured by our bad temper." [23] The boy had by this time been sent to Stowe.
Wanting to visit him "in his new setting," Wells inquired: "Will you let me know precisely how he
stands at Stowe? Is he known to be your son? My
son? Who knows what?" [24] Wells was also insistent
that Anthony should visit Easton Glebe.[25] He had
never in the past paid any attention to Anthony's
Christmas, but just before the holidays in 1928 he
asked the boy to Easton Glebe. Rebecca declined this
belated invitation, since American friends were loan-
ing their attractive flat in Paris to Anthony and herself, but offered to send him down for New Year's
eve. Wells's response was intemperate, even for him.
"I think your refusal to let Anthony go to Easton for
Christmas one of the most malicious things you have
ever done," he told her. "He loses the chance of getting upon jolly terms with his half brothers, he loses a
bright time. For a mere whim of yours." [26]

These recriminations can only have confirmed Rebecca in her decision to proceed with a plan which
her solicitor Theobald (later Sir Theobald) Mathew
of Messrs. Charles Russell had suggested to her. If
she legally adopted Anthony, she would be able to
show his adoption certificate rather than his birth
certificate, and this would spare him trouble and humiliation, particularly with regard to school authori-
ties. Having secured Wells's acquiescence, as she
thought, she told Mathew to institute adoption proceedings in January of 1929.[27] Anthony signified his
willingness to be adopted. Rebecca answered the
schedule of questions put to her by the Official Solicitor. Her friends Lady Rhondda and Sir James Mel-

ville gave supporting testimony. The adoption order was to have come before the judge for decision on 18 March, but on that day Mathew had regretfully to report "a hitch." [28] Wells had after all instructed Messrs. Gedge, Fiske, and Gedge to oppose the adoption.

The judge adjourned the case until Wells could return from Provence. Meanwhile, he was pressing Rebecca for an explanation of Anthony's lack of progress at school. During the boy's visit to Easton Glebe in the early spring, he was given a letter for Rebecca in which Wells "asked for certain points about his standing at Stowe." When this information was not provided, Wells made difficulties about paying Anthony's school bills and threatened to "go to Roxburgh . . . and discuss the whole situation with him." [29] By the time the adoption finally came before the judge in early June, Wells and Rebecca were on terms of extreme hostility. Neither was present at this *in camera* hearing, though Rebecca was at hand in case the judge desired to see her. Wells's counsel asked the court to grant the adoption only if certain conditions were met. At the same time Wells's solicitor told Mathew that Rebecca was supposed to be "living a frivolous life among a circle of idle second-rate friends," naming five persons, only one of whom (a lady of perfect respectability) was known to Anthony. When he went on to remark to Mathew, "I can't blame Wells, it must be distressing for him to see the boy being brought up with all these seedy people," Mathew replied, "Well, the particular seedy friends of hers that I know are the Master of the Rolls and his Wife." Such allegations could not have been made in court, of course, where Wells's liaison with Odette would have provided an unanswerable rejoinder.

The judge was Mr. Justice Clausen, a moral precisionist of the old school who was later to decide for Arnold Bennett's widow, long separated from her husband, in a suit for possession of the manuscript journals which Bennett had given to the mistress with whom he was living. He granted the adoption only with an accompanying compulsory order that Rebecca should consult with Wells about Anthony's education, allow him to spend part of his holidays with Wells, and designate Wells as his guardian in the event of her death. The first two conditions were already being met, and Rebecca perforce accepted the third, though with profound foreboding. She added a codicil to her will making Wells Anthony's guardian, and on 24 June Mathew was able to inform her "that at long last the adoption order has been made." [30] But her resentment of Wells's obstructiveness remained undiminished, and she was profoundly hurt by the allegations against her way of life that had been reported to her.

Wells was not slow in claiming his rights. He visited Anthony at Stowe, thereby causing something of a stir at the school, and during the ensuing vacation he insisted that the boy and his tutor spend three weeks in September at Easton Glebe. Since Rebecca had taken a villa at Agay on the then unfrequented coastline between Cannes and St. Raphael, in the department of Var, for the summer expressly to enable Anthony to swim, she was indignant at this demand. She believed that he would see little of Wells. "He cannot possibly have Anthony at his beck and call unless he accepts full responsibility," she wrote to Mathew. "I do not wander off during his holidays and return just for weekends, and I disapprove of the company he is left in in the intervals." [31] She accordingly urged Anthony to ask Wells to let him remain on the Riviera and defer his visit until Christmas. [32] Wells prevailed, however, and Anthony was sent to Easton Glebe in early September. There was the usual confusion about arrangements for Anthony's trip and reception at Easton Glebe, which Rebecca attributed to muddle and ill-will at Wells's end. "I terribly long for him to commit himself to the stage where I could again refuse to communicate with him," she confided to Mathew. [33]

With these frustrations fresh in her mind, Rebecca brooded over the threat to Anthony's welfare that she saw in Wells's new role as his guardian. She finally asked Bertrand Russell to serve also in this capacity. After rehearsing her earlier history with Wells, she noted in her letter that the past months had "shown him quite unbalanced."

> He went down to Stowe before the term ended and created more trouble, and has removed Anthony to Easton from this perfectly lovely villa for the last three weeks of his holidays. (The boy adores him. I've always brought him up to do so, which I rather regret now.) This has all been done with an extraordinary and insane air of a saint struggling with the per-

sonification of evil. He has shown in every way
of late the most extraordinary unwillingness to
let anybody have their own way.

Rebecca feared that if she were to die Wells "would
get bored with the boy, and would get his fun by
frustrating him at any crisis." It was this alarming
prospect which caused her to ask Russell to serve
with Wells as testamentary guardian. "H. G. is afraid
of you," she told him, "and wouldn't dare to oppose
you or do anything in your sight that was manifestly
reactionary." [34] When nothing came of her appeal,
which Rebecca afterwards saw as "ghastly" in the
self-humiliation it entailed, she chose Mathew as
Anthony's co-guardian.

   Meanwhile, Wells had given Rebecca fresh cause
for offense by sending her a telegram telling her
that she must return at once from Var to take Anthony to his lung specialist and dentist. Rebecca had
sent full information about these appointments; Easton Glebe was an easy train or car journey from London; and the house was stocked with a secretary and
servants who could take Anthony to the city. Hence
she disregarded this arbitrary summons. A further
telegram and insulting letters followed, but for once
Wells seems to have felt that he had gone too far. At
any rate he wrote Rebecca with unexpected cordial-
ity about her just published *Harriet Hume*. This
highly stylized novel may strike the reader of today
as somewhat mannered and insubstantial, but Wells
discovered in its narrative of the intermittent encounters of two lovers in a dreamlike London many
echoes of the fantasies that he and Rebecca had

played out together in happier days. He also found it interesting that the "love-antagonism" of Harriet Hume and Arnold Condover paralleled Jung's "ideas about the *persona, anima* and *animus,*" which he was then studying. Concerning the novel generally, he wrote:

> You've got your distinctive fantasy and humour into it, and it gives play for just the peculiar intricate wittiness which is one of your most delightful and inimitable characteristics. It is just as though you were coming awake and alive after years in a sort of intellectual trance. It's a joy to praise you unreservedly. Homage and admiration.[35]

The winter of 1929/30 passed without overt friction except for Wells's renewed complaints about Anthony's lack of progress at Stowe. Even here he was at least willing to accept joint responsibility. "This isn't a report for *us* to be proud of," he wrote to Rebecca.[36] Indeed, having had his way, Wells was no longer in a mood to be vindictive. When an uneasy encounter with Rebecca in March brought home to him how much he had hurt her, he did his best to make reparations:

> I'm very heavy hearted about you. Very sorry indeed to think I've worried and wounded you. I'll try to consider you more in the future. I didn't think you and I could ever meet without laughter but there wasn't much last night. I think you have rather an exceptional power of diffusing highly refractive mists about you and

seeing things in the wrong proportions. Probably you never realized how much I was in love with you and what a bitter and sorrowful thing it was to lose your companionship. Nor can you know how much you have humiliated me in the past. And exasperated me. I'm not recriminating, but I wish you could realize that I was very deeply your lover and that you made me suffer pretty badly. Even now not to see you well distresses me. When you score any success I say, which is absurd: "That's *my* Panther." [37]

Seeking to dispel what he called Rebecca's "queer fancies," [38] he had his solicitor confer with Mathew about the best way of reassuring her concerning the allegations about her way of life made at the time of the adoption hearing. The upshot was a letter in which Fiske asserted to Mathew:

We saw our Client to-day, and are very sorry to hear from him that your Client appears to have an idea that when before the Judge, our Counsel made some remarks reflecting upon her character or mode of life. I was present at the hearings, and nothing, I am quite sure, was said which might in any way reflect upon your Client in any manner whatever. I remember that our Counsel did say that your Client, in carrying out her literary or journalistic activities, might have to be abroad in New York or Paris for some considerable time, and therefore it would be an advantage for the boy to have a home at Easton to which he could go at times, but I am quite sure these journeys were only referred to as being

for your Client's professional purposes, and
there was not the slightest idea of there being
any insinuation made against her in any other
way, and as for the names of any other party or
parties being mentioned, I can absolutely deny
that our Counsel ever did so.[39]

These assurances were beside the point, if not actually disingenuous, since the remarks to which Rebecca objected had been made, not by counsel in
court, but by Wells's solicitor to Rebecca's.

The two years that had begun with Anthony's
illness were in fact the nadir of Rebecca's relationship with Wells. The care of a sick boy, her own
ill health, her constant fatigue, and her worry about
money combined to make life difficult, but worse still
was that she saw as Wells's motiveless malignity, his
willingness to inflict pain on her for no apparent
reason. His earlier behavior had been comprehensible. "After all, I was there. H. G. could have
reacted to me, but later I was not there, it was such
long-distance cruelty." Rebecca was also disturbed by
the effect that contact with Easton Glebe might have
on Anthony. She disapproved of "the imitation life
of a country gentleman without any of the responsi-
bilities of a normal landowner" that Wells lived
there. She deplored the preoccupation with material
things that Easton Glebe was likely to encourage in
the boy and the habits of extravagance that he might
acquire. She felt that he set out for each visit "with
an air of telling me that they didn't want me in that
glamorous world of Easton, but they did want
[him]," not realizing that for Rebecca Easton Glebe

was "a plague spot and a horror, from which I had fled half across the world." [40] Yet she could not put the situation in perspective for Anthony without attacking his father, and this she would not do.

Rebecca was under no such restraint in dealing with Wells himself, and from time to time she told him some home truths. The day-to-day responsibility for Anthony's welfare was hers. Wells merely intervened casually in his life, at long intervals and usually with disruptive consequences. When they exchanged letters about Anthony's admittedly unsuccessful schooling during his visit to Lou Pidou at the end of 1931, she offered this summary of Wells's relationship to his son:

> As for the educational business, I don't quite like your tone. "I've interfered with little in his education so far because I have trusted to your love for and pride in him." Gammon and spinach! You interfered very little because you couldn't be bothered. I have in my time received a large number of letters from you, and when I was going through them not long ago . . . I was struck by the very large number which referred to Anthony with indifference and hostility. A letter written when Anthony was six months old upbraiding me for not letting him be adopted by someone, on the ground that you found it so boring to come and see me in a country house where there was no tennis-court. Letters expressing rage because I had to look after Anthony because his school was closed for mumps. Let-

ters in answer to three of mine begging you to
let me remove Anthony from St. Piran's because
I thought he was unhappy, expressing complete
indifference and saying Anthony was not worth
while taking any trouble over. A letter in answer
to mine saying that I must stay in America because
my contract had been interrupted by illness and
I had to stay on an extra month, and asking you
to go and see Anthony, refusing on the ground
that you had been to see him once, and could
not be bothered to go again. The financial letters, showing how you grudged every penny of
yours or even mine that was spent on Anthony,
are also interesting. . . .

I must ask you, for Anthony's sake, to make
all suggestions [about his schooling] through
me. I know that it will irritate you to hear it, but
the fact is that both in regard to Anthony's public school and University education several people of acknowledged standing have refused to
have anything to do with Anthony because it
might involve them in correspondence with you.
Doubtless this feeling is very unjust, but we cannot hold up Anthony's education till we remove
it.

I know this letter will offend you, and I
grieve, for though I know you are a great hum-
bug I also know you're a great man.[41]

The sense of being altogether out of Wells's power
to which this letter bears witness reflects a significant
change in Rebecca's circumstances. In 1930 she had

married Henry Maxwell Andrews. What this meant
to her is suggested by a letter she wrote to S. K.
Ratcliffe before the ceremony:

> 1928—owing to Anthony's illness—and 1929
> owing to a more hideous, malevolent and useless
> threat—were the worst years I have had up till
> now. If I had no happiness to look forward to I
> would want the wedding as a sign of gratitude to
> Henry for what his feeling for me during the
> last year has done to build me up.[42]

Settled at last in a happy and orderly existence, Rebecca was soon embarked on the notable career as a
writer which lay ahead of her during the second half
of her life, and her brushes with Wells could no
longer devastate her as they had in the past. For the
next few years the two maintained a sort of armed
truce which survived several trying episodes. When
Wells wrote disparagingly about Rebecca for the
Hearst press in America, she followed Mathew's advice and took no notice of his baiting.[43] Next came a
crisis in Anthony's life. He had departed from Stowe
and was being tutored privately when Odette asked
him to spend the Christmas season of 1931 with
Wells and herself at Lou Pidou. The visit was a disaster, though from no fault of Anthony's, and it resulted in an uneasy silence which was no bad thing at
that particular juncture. Moreover, when Anthony
for a time stopped seeing his father, much of the
reason for tension between Wells and Rebecca disappeared. After Wells and Odette separated, he was
briefly resentful because *Time and Tide*, of which Rebecca's friend Lady Rhondda was the proprietor,

published in 1934 a series of articles by Odette attacking him,[44] but his irritation soon passed.

By the end of that year, Wells and Rebecca were ready to meet again. He took the initiative by writing from Menton for a copy of her new book of short stories, *The Harsh Voice*.[45] When it came, he had high praise for the workmanship of three or four of the tales. He was particularly impressed by "The Life Sentence." Concerning "Salt of the Earth," which he mistakenly assumed to be a study of her sister, he told her: "I'm glad you've killed Letty. If she had been killed ages ago the world might have been very different." And he tried once more to state the conflict between his mind and Rebecca's:

> From the point of view of work it is well we got away from each other. Our intellectual quality is so different that I should always have nagged you by trying to clip your extravagant black pinions and you would have always been bothered by my search for the crude and bare and commonplace. You have a richness. I am simplicity. That is why I came off artistically from the beginning and got slovenly later and why you had to begin with such a spate of undisciplined imagination in the *Judge* before you got to the MASTERY of these stories.[46]

From 1935 onwards Wells and Rebecca were on increasingly cordial terms. Even at the time when he was treating her with a vindictiveness that in her eyes approached insanity, Rebecca did not forget the charming companion whom she had loved. As old age overtook him, the deep affection that they had always felt for each other rose unimpeded to the surface. In Rebecca's view this concluding phase of easy friendship became possible largely through the slow readjustment in Wells's emotional life which followed Jane's death. His responses had been fixed in the pattern of "the enslaved sexual woman being sacrificed to the Great White Virgin-Mother, but when Jane disappeared there was nobody to offer up the sexual woman to—there was therefore no point in rebuking me for having walked off the stage. The whole performance was at an end." This cooling process did not progress very far while Wells was with Odette, but the "comfortable and undemanding relationships" that he enjoyed with the ladies who followed her and the efficient care with which Gip's wife Marjorie looked after him brought some reason and order into his life. Moreover, it became a strong bond of sympathy between Wells and Rebecca that both forcefully opposed English appeasement of the Nazis and that Henry Andrews worked courageously for Jews and liberals in Germany during the many visits to that country which his business necessitated. At any rate, Wells and Rebecca came once more to see each other frequently. During the Second World War, when she was living in the country and he in London, she constantly took food parcels to him. Near the end of his life, indeed, he reminded her "with a Falstaffian wink that throughout the war he had never gone without bacon and eggs for his breakfast." [47]

Wells died on 13 August 1946. Rebecca and Anthony were present at his cremation three days later. She wrote afterwards to Marjorie Wells, the person in his family to whom she felt closest, that she had picked the very day on which that ceremony occurred to bring to London for Wells to look at some pictures of "the deflated Nazis" at Nuremberg, where she had been reporting the war trials. Had his death not intervened, she would also have told him of her conversations with a high American official who had spoken of "his youth and what H. G. had done for his mind in the narrow society of very wealthy people." Later in the letter she wrote:

> I loved him all my life and always will, and I bitterly reproach myself for not having stayed with him, because I think I was fairly good for him. But you know the reverse of the medal, the tyranny that was the incorrigible part of him. I could not have submitted to it all my life—nor do I think that he could have loved me or that I could have loved him if I had been the kind of person that could. And indeed he got on pretty well without me.[48]

Considering this valediction twenty-eight years afterwards, Rebecca saw in it the mixture of good sense and nonsense engendered by grief. It was ridiculous for her to reproach herself for having left Wells, but it is also true that she never ceased to love him only a little less than she loved her husband, and that he in fact got on pretty well without her.

The principal manuscript sources of this book are Wells's letters to Dame Rebecca West and her few surviving letters to him in the Beinecke Library at Yale University. Where no location is given below for quotations from manuscripts, they are from this collection. The use of these letters is restricted, as is the use of the much larger archive of Dame Rebecca's papers of which they are a part. I have also drawn on other letters at Yale, in the Wells Archive at the University of Illinois, in the possession of Professor G. P. Wells, and in my own collection. These are specifically identified below. The text of Wells's letters is literal, except that I have replaced ampersands with *and*s and added apostrophes and minimal punctuation where needed. Quotations from Wells's writings, published and unpublished, are made with the permission of his literary executors.

As I noted in my preface, Dame Rebecca read and commented on several successive drafts of my narrative. The subjects dealt with at length in her statements are identified at the beginning of the notes to individual chapters. I have also drawn on three significant earlier documents which Dame Rebecca has given to me: typed extracts from her diary of 1944, a draft letter of that year concerning her life with Wells, and a briefer account of the same topic written in 1957. Quotations from her letters and other writings are made with her permission.

I am indebted to Professor G. Evelyn Hutchinson for his *Preliminary List of the Writings of Rebecca West, 1912–1951* (New Haven, 1957). It may be mentioned that he and Mr. William Keller are preparing an enlarged edition of this bibliography. I am particularly grateful also to Miss Frances Taylor for unusually demanding secretarial services and to Mrs. Ellen Graham, my thorough and efficient editor at the Yale University Press.

Chapter I

Dame Rebecca's statements of 1971 and 1973
(her family and early life)

1 "Marriage," *Freewoman,* 19 September 1912.
2 The quotations in the preceding three paragraphs are from *The Fountain Overflows* (London, 1970), pp. 249, 299, 127, 256, 134, 215, 36, 77, 418. Rebecca's novel *The Judge* (London, 1922) is dedicated to her mother. The portrait of Mrs. Melville in Book I seems to be drawn in large part from her. See particularly Ellen Melville's reflections at Mrs. Melville's death bed, pp. 180–97.
3 "A Training in Truculence," *Clarion,* 14 February 1913.
4 "A Modern Crusader," *Freewoman,* 23 May 1912.
5 "A Training in Truculence," *Clarion,* 14 February 1913.
6 *The Fountain Overflows,* p. 336.
7 "A Training in Truculence," *Clarion,* 14 February 1913.
8 "The Prig in Power," *Clarion,* 10 January 1913.
9 Rebecca noted in the *Clarion* on 17 October 1913 that she had been writing about the suffrage movement "on and off for seven years."
10 Cicely [*sic*] Fairfield, "The Position of Women in India," *Freewoman,* 30 November 1911.
11 Rebecca, interviewed by Anthony Curtis, *Listener,* 15 February 1973, p. 211.
12 "The Gospel According to Mrs. Humphry Ward," *Freewoman,* 15 February 1912.
13 *The Fountain Overflows,* p. 122.

14   "The True Traveller," *Freewoman,* 2 May 1912.
15   "The Gospel According to Granville Barker," *Freewoman,* 7 March 1912.
16   "The Belief in Personal Immortality," *New Freewoman,* 15 July 1913.
17   " 'Elsie Lindtner,' " *Freewoman,* 13 June 1912.

Chapter II

1   *Freewoman,* 7 December 1911.
2   *Freewoman,* 23 May 1912.
3   "English Literature, 1880–1905," *Freewoman,* 25 July 1912.
4   *H. G. Wells and His Family* (Edinburgh, 1955), p. 112.
5   *The Fountain Overflows,* p. 375.
6   Mrs. Townshend to Rebecca, 24 July 1914. "Indissoluble Matrimony" was published in *Blast,* I (1914), 98–117.
7   "The Sterner Sex," *Clarion,* 18 July 1913.
8   The date of this letter is established by the last sentence. Mrs. Wells left Switzerland for London on 5 February 1913, and had returned to Little Easton Rectory by 12 February (Meyer, *H. G. Wells and His Family,* p. 121).
9   This information came to Rebecca when she visited "Elizabeth" at her house in Provence many years later.
10   "Trees of Gold," *New Freewoman,* 15 June 1913.
11   "At Valladolid," *New Freewoman,* 1 August 1913.
12   "Two Plays by Tchekof," *Freewoman,* 11 April 1912.
13   Wells to Rebecca, late May 1913.
14   Wells to Rebecca, early June 1913.
15   Rebecca to Wells, June 1913. Of the two attempts at suicide mentioned in this letter, Dame Rebecca later wrote: "I think it would have been a miracle if they had succeeded, although I meant them to, in the double-think way of youth."
16   Wells to Rebecca, June 1913.

Chapter III

1   Wells to Rebecca, 14 January 1914.
2   Wells to Rebecca, early July 1913.
3   "Nana," *New Freewoman,* 1 July 1913.
4   *New Freewoman,* 15 June 1913.
5   "The Life of Emily Davison," *Clarion,* 20 June 1913.
6   "A Quiet Day with the Constitutionals," *Clarion,* 1 August 1913.

7   "On Mentioning the Unmentionable," *Clarion*, 26 September 1913.
8   The same.
9   "Lynch Law," *Clarion*, 17 October 1913.
10 "English Literature, 1880–1905," *Freewoman*, 25 July 1912.
11 "Every Home a Little Earlswood," *Clarion*, 7 March 1913.
12 "Another Book Which Ought Not to Have Been Written," *Clarion*, 21 November 1913.
13 Wells to Rebecca, 4 October 1913.
14 Wells to Rebecca, 20 October 1913.
15 Wells to Rebecca, October 1913.
16 "The Fool and the Wise Man," *New Freewoman*, 1 October 1913.
17 Wells to Rebecca, 18 and 28 October 1913.
18 Wells to Rebecca, 2 November 1913.
19 *Clarion*, 14 November 1913.

Chapter IV

1   Their child, Anthony Panther West, was born on 4 August 1914, prematurely it would seem. In a letter of 13 February 1914 Wells speaks of the baby being expected in September.
2   Wells to Rebecca, 2 December 1913.
3   Wells to Rebecca, early December 1913.
4   Wells to Rebecca, early December 1913.
5   Wells to Rebecca, 17 December 1913.
6   "Two Plays by Tchekof," *Freewoman*, 11 April 1912.
7   *Works*, 28 volumes (London, 1924–27), XIX, 140, 163–64.
8   Wells to Rebecca, 14 January 1914.
9   "A Training in Truculence," *Clarion*, 14 February 1913.
10 *The Fountain Overflows*, p. 375.
11 A deduction from the fact that Amanda, Rebecca's counterpart in *The Research Magnificent*, originates the comparable names there.
12 *The Fountain Overflows*, p. 375.
13 "Autumn," *Clarion*, 4 April 1913.
14 Wells to Rebecca, December 1913.
15 Wells to Rebecca, 6 December 1913.
16 Wells to Rebecca, 14 January 1914.
17 From Wells's letters to Rebecca of December 1913.
18 Wells to Rebecca, 23 December 1913.
19 *Clarion*, 28 November 1913.

20 An undated letter from Wells which clearly refers to one of
    Rebecca's three final contributions. That of 28 November is
    the only possibility since by 2 December Wells was signing
    his letters "Jaguar" and this is signed "H. G."
21 *Clarion*, 5 December 1913.
22 *Clarion*, 12 December 1913.

Chapter V

1   Wells to Rebecca, 31 December 1913.
2   Wells to Rebecca, 14 January 1914.
3   Wells to Rebecca, 14 January 1914.
4   Wells to Rebecca, late January 1914.
5   Wells to Rebecca, late January 1914.
6   Wells to Rebecca, late January 1914.
7   Wells to Rebecca, late January 1914.
8   Wells to Rebecca, early February 1914.
9   Wells to Rebecca, early February 1914.
10 Wells to Rebecca, early February 1914.
11 Wells to Rebecca, 15? February 1914.
12 Wells to Rebecca, 17 February 1914.
13 Wells to Rebecca, mid-February 1914.
14 Wells to Rebecca, 1 March 1914.
15 Rebecca West, "Women of England," *Atlantic Monthly*, Jan-
    uary 1916. In the course of this article Rebecca relates the
    wartime experiences of a couple not unlike Wells and her-
    self, describing briefly their residences at Hunstanton,
    Braughing, and Alderton.
16 Wells to Rebecca, 4 July 1914.
17 Wells to Rebecca, mid-August 1914.
18 Wells to Robert Ross, July? 1914 (copy, Illinois).
19 These reviews will be recorded in the new edition of Mr.
    Hutchinson's bibliography.
20 Wells to Rebecca, 13 June 1914.
21 Wells to Rebecca, 19 May 1914.
22 Wells to Rebecca, 14 April 1914.
23 Wells to Rebecca, 3 March 1914.
24 Wells to Rebecca, 12 June 1914.
25 Wells to Rebecca, July? 1914.
26 Wells to Rebecca, 2? and 3 August 1914.
27 "Women of England," *Atlantic Monthly*, January 1916, p. 7.
28 Jane Wells to Wells, 4 August 1914.

29   Wells to Rebecca, 5 August 1914.
30   Wells to Rebecca, 6? August 1914.
31   Wells to Rebecca, 7 August 1914.
32   Wells to Rebecca, early August 1914.
33   Wells to Rebecca, early July 1914.
34   Wells to Rebecca, 23 August 1914.
35   Wells to Rebecca, 23 August 1914.
36   Wells to Rebecca, 30 August 1914.
37   Mrs. Townshend to Wells, 18 August 1914.
38   Wells to Rebecca, mid-September 1914.

Chapter VI

Dame Rebecca's statements of 1971
(Mrs. Morse and her other servants) and 1973 (Alderton)

 1   "Women of England," *Atlantic Monthly,* January 1916, pp. 8–11.
 2   Wells to Rebecca, October? 1914.
 3   Wells to Rebecca, mid-September 1914.
 4   Wells to Robert Ross, late 1914 (copy, Illinois).
 5   Wells to Jane Wells, late 1914 (Illinois).
 6   Wells to Rebecca, December? 1914.
 7   Wells to Rebecca, 15 April 1915.
 8   Wells to Rebecca, April? 1915.
 9   Wells to Rebecca, April? 1915.
10   "Women of England," *Atlantic Monthly,* January 1916, p. 10.
11   Wells to Rebecca, 22 June 1915.
12   Wells to Rebecca, April? 1915.
13   "Women of England," *Atlantic Monthly,* January 1916, p. 11.
14   Wells to Rebecca, June 1915.
15   As is witnessed by an affectionate note written by her to Rebecca on Anthony's fourth birthday, 4 August 1918.
16   Rebecca to S. K. Ratcliffe, 4 February 1916 (Yale).
17   Wells to Rebecca, 4 May 1916.
18   Wells to Rebecca, 8 October 1915.
19   Wells to Rebecca, late November 1915.
20   Wells to Rebecca, late April? 1916.
21   Wells to Rebecca, May 1916.
22   See *Experiment in Autobiography,* 2 volumes (London, 1934), I, 112–25.
23   *The Return of the Soldier* (London, 1918), pp. 66–67.
24   Wells to Rebecca, 20 August 1916.

25 Wells to Rebecca, September 1916.
26 Wells to Rebecca, 17 September 1916.
27 Rebecca to Wells, 18? September, and Wells to Rebecca, 19 September 1916.
28 Wells to Rebecca, 21 September 1916.

Chapter VII

Dame Rebecca's statement of 1971
(the bombings at Leigh, Miss North)

1   Wells to Rebecca, 23 March 1917.
2   Wells to Rebecca, 19 May 1917.
3   Wells to Rebecca, 13 September 1917.
4   Rebecca to the author, 1973.
5   *The Fountain Overflows,* p. 229.
6   Wells to Rebecca, mid-September 1917.
7   Wells to Rebecca, late September 1917.
8   Wells to Rebecca, late September 1917.
9   Wells to Colles, 15 June 1914 (Illinois).
10 I should note that Dame Rebecca explicitly disavows the interpretation of her novel which follows. She wrote to me on 14 July 1971: "As for 'The Return of the Soldier,' you give a most brilliant explanation of what must have been at the back of my mind, but it was not at the front of my mind. The story was written round the personality of Mrs. Vernon, a very nice woman, who was our landlady at Claverton Street over several years, whom I had come across some years earlier because an American friend of mine had had rooms in her house. She was the complete Margaret, and she had once been to Monkey Island on an unspecified occasion, which was of great importance to her, and speculations on what this might have been gave me the idea for the story. Kitty is not at all my idea of Jane. She was not nearly as good-looking as Jane, who was remarkably pretty even into her middle years, but she was much more of the Establishment. Jane had no look of accustomed luxury, though she had another kind of charm, and she had also a look of determination which was amusing on some one who was so faint in colour and so immobile. The original of Kitty was a woman I met only once, when someone took me to a house said to be the original of the house Galsworthy de-

scribes as being built by Bosinney for Soames in the Forsyte Saga." If I persist in my interpretation it is in the conviction that this is an instance to which D. H. Lawrence's injunction, believe the tale, not the teller, applies.

11 *The Return of the Soldier,* pp. 102–03. This novel was begun in the winter of 1915/16, though it was not published until two years later.

12 Rebecca, statement of 1957 (Ray).

13 *The Return of the Soldier,* p. 39.

14 The same, pp. 51–52.

15 The same, pp. 14, 85.

16 The same, pp. 130–31.

17 The same, p. 159.

18 The same, pp. 162–67.

19 The same, p. 188.

Chapter VIII

Dame Rebecca's statements of 1972
(*Cornwall, Capri*) and 1973 (*Amalfi*)

1 Wells to Rebecca, 1918?.

2 Hardy to Wells, January 1919.

3 Wells to Rebecca, 6 March 1920.

4 Shaw to Wells, 3 October 1921.

5 Wells to Rebecca, letters of 1920.

6 *The Secret Places of the Heart, Works,* XXV, v, 407–15, 510–13, 545, 553–54, 564–68.

7 Rebecca, typescript of 1944 diary (Ray).

8 Wells to Rebecca, late October 1920.

9 Wells to Rebecca, 20 November 1920.

10 Wells to Rebecca, November 1920.

11 Wells to Rebecca, late November 1920.

12 Wells to Rebecca, December 1920.

13 Wells to Rebecca, 20 December 1920 and early January 1921.

14 Wells to Rebecca, 10 January 1921.

15 Wells to Rebecca, late April 1921.

16 Wells to Rebecca, 17 April 1921.

17 Wells to Rebecca, 30 April 1921.

18 Wells to Rebecca, summer 1921.

19 These drawings were made between August and October 1921.

20 Wells to Rebecca, summer 1921.
21 Wells to Rebecca, 19–27 October 1921.
22 Wells to Rebecca, late December 1921.
23 Wells to Rebecca, ca. 10 November 1921.

Chapter IX

Dame Rebecca's statements of 1972
(Algeciras, Spain, Paris, and Porlock)

1 Wells to Rebecca, 20 March 1922.
2 Rebecca, typescript of diary, 5 April 1944 (Ray).
3 Wells to Rebecca, July? 1922.
4 Wells to Rebecca, August 1922.
5 The quotations in this and the following paragraphs are from Wells's letters to Rebecca of August 1922, none of which is dated.
6 These two letters, which are also undated, may probably be assigned to September 1922.

Chapter X

Dame Rebecca's statements of 1972 and 1973
(the last phase of the
Frau Gatternigg affair, Marienbad)

1 As is noted above, Wells destroyed nearly all of Rebecca's letters to him. Several of her other early correspondences have also perished. It seems useful, then, to give here the full text of a letter at Yale which she wrote to S. K. Ratcliffe on 21 March 1923 about her dream of a trip to America as a way out of her impasse with Wells. The reader will see how entirely it confirms her recollections of a half-century later: "What is this story that I hear from Lettie about a moral lady in Boston who is making hell about me? I heard something of it today from her but she seemed not very definite. I wish you would tell me exactly how bad it is. It is for various reasons an extraordinarily embittering piece of news. I may as well tell you exactly why. I have had an appalling life with H. G. during the last five years, due partly to domestic difficulties arising out of our relationship, partly to an increasing nervous instability on his part, which leads to long periods which begin with fits of almost mania-

cal rage and then end in weeks on end of childish depen-
dence. I had for instance two months of last year with him
in Spain when for only ten days could he be described as
normal. I have stuck to him partly for his own sake—mainly
for Anthony's sake—but really quite a lot for his own sake
as he has, to an extent nobody quite realises, not a soul on
earth who looks after him. I have however increasingly felt
that I cannot go on—for one thing I cannot spend most of
my time sick nursing while I also have to keep an eye on
Anthony *and* do my work, and I can assure you I am getting
no adequate financial recompense. Also I am getting (as is
natural from a person in such a neurotic state) no gratitude
whatsoever. I feel that perhaps if I could go on it would be
my duty to do so. But I can't. I'm sleepless and collapsing
physically in strange ways—my feet and ankles swell until I
feel sick half the time—and I can't do it. I have tried to
leave H. G. innumerable times, but never without his following me and asking me to come back. I have as a matter
of fact left him at the moment but I am dreading another
attempt to get me to come back. It is also as I have a steady
monogamous nature and would have been the most wifely
wife on earth extremely difficult not to take the job again.
My only hope therefore of getting and keeping clear is to
get to America! Therefore this news does depress me. I
would be glad if you would tell me all about it. I have a
book (about 30,000 words) in my head, 'Second Thoughts
on Feminism,' which I could write, if I keep free, in 2,000
word articles, which would make it plain where I stood and
how unlikely it was that I should preach anything too revo-
lutionary. But I suppose the antagonistic feeling is purely
personal and can't be overcome. Well, I will come to
America in any case, just to look around and write a bit."

2   Wells to Rebecca, 21 March 1923.
3   Wells to Rebecca, both late March 1923.
4   Wells to Rebecca, early April 1923.
5   Wells to Rebecca, April 1923.
6   Wells to Frau Duchinsky, 23 June and 8 July 1922 (Ray).
7   Wells to Frau Gatternigg, November and 25 December
    1922 (Ray).
8   Wells to Frau Gatternigg, 7 February 1923, and Wells to
    Anatole France, presumably of the same date (Ray).
9   Wells to Rebecca, 26 June 1923.
10 *New York Times,* 23 June 1923. The British Museum's news-

paper depository has only the 6:30 edition of the *Star* for 21 June. This edition does not contain the story.

11 Wells to Rebecca, 4 July 1923.
12 Rebecca, draft letter of 1944.
13 Wells to Rebecca, 4 July 1923.
14 Wells to Frau Duchinsky (Ray). This letter is dated 24 October 1920, possibly not in Wells's hand, but it clearly belongs to 1923. *Men Like Gods* was serialized in the *Westminster Gazette* between December 1922 and February 1923.
15 Wells to Rebecca, 3 July 1923.
16 Wells to Rebecca, early July 1923.
17 Wells to Rebecca, 9 July 1923.
18 Wells to Rebecca, December 1923.

Chapter XI

Dame Rebecca's statements of 1972 (St. Piran's)
and 1973 (her experiences in the United States)

1   Wells to Rebecca, December 1923.
2   Wells to Rebecca, undated but both fall 1923.
3   Wells to Rebecca, 11 November 1923.
4   Wells to Rebecca, 15 November 1923.
5   Wells to Rebecca, 19 November 1923.
6   Wells to Rebecca, 26 November 1923.
7   Wells to Rebecca, 27 November 1923.
8   Wells to Rebecca, 15 December 1923.
9   Wells to Rebecca, 9 January 1924.
10 Wells to Rebecca, 8 January 1924.
11 Wells to Rebecca, 9 January 1924.
12 Wells to Rebecca, 18 February 1924.
13 Rebecca to S. K. Ratcliffe, 25 November 1923 (Yale).
14 Wells to Rebecca, 4 June 1924.
15 Wells to Rebecca, 4 June 1924.
16 Wells to Rebecca, 28 June 1924.
17 Wells to Rebecca, 3 August 1924.
18 Wells to Rebecca, 23 August 1924.
19 Wells to Rebecca, 24 August 1924.
20 Wells to Rebecca, 9 December 1924.
21 Wells, *The Research Magnificent* (London, 1926), p. 258.
22 The same, pp. 180, 316, 277, 241, 271, 274. Rebecca liked *The Research Magnificent*. See her review, "Novel of Ideas,"

New Republic, supplement to the issue of 20 November 1915, pp. 3–5.

23 "In a sense Helen has been exorcised here in Provence; I can hardly trace how; but the scars are fresh and plain" (*The World of William Clissold,* 2 vols., New York, 1926, II, 494).

24 The same, II, 494.

25 The same, II, 495–96.

26 The same, II, 499–500.

27 The same, II, 501.

28 The same, II, 502.

29 The same, II, 508–09.

30 The same, II, 501.

Chapter XII

Dame Rebecca's statements of 1973

1   Rebecca to Bertrand Russell, early September 1929.

2   Wells to Rebecca, 9 January 1924.

3   Rebecca to Bertrand Russell, early September 1929.

4   Wells to Rebecca, 23 August 1924.

5   Wells to Rebecca, 30 October 1924.

6   Wells to Rebecca, 10 December 1926.

7   Wells to Rebecca, 12 July 1926.

8   Wells to Rebecca, 1 October 1927.

9   Wells to Rebecca, 3 December 1927.

10 Wells to Rebecca, 16 November 1927.

11 Wells to Rebecca, 3 January 1928.

12 Rebecca to Wells, 7 January 1928.

13 Wells to Rebecca, 2 March 1928.

14 Rebecca to Mrs. Richards, 11 May 1928.

15 Wells to Rebecca, 2 May 1928.

16 Wells to Rebecca, mid-June 1928.

17 Rebecca West, *The Strange Necessity* (London, 1928), pp. 199–200.

18 Wells to Rebecca, 17 July 1928.

19 Wells to Rebecca, late July 1928.

20 Wells to Rebecca, 26 July 1928.

21 Wells to Rebecca, 3 August 1928. "Big Thinks" is an allusion to the following passage in chapter 21 of *The Island of Doctor Moreau:* "The Ape Man bored me however. He assumed, on the strength of his five digits, that he was my equal, and was forever jabbering at me, jabbering the most

arrant nonsense. One thing about him entertained me a little: he had a fantastic trick of coining new words. He had an idea, I believe, that to gabble about names that meant nothing was the proper use of speech. He called it 'big thinks,' to distinguish it from 'little thinks'—the sane everyday interests of life. If ever I made a remark he did not understand, he would praise it very much, ask me to say it again, learn it by heart, and go off repeating it, with a word wrong here or there, to all the milder of the Beast People. He thought nothing of what was plain and comprehensible. I invented some very curious 'big thinks' for his especial use. I think now that he was the silliest creature I ever met; he had developed in the most wonderful way the distinctive silliness of man without losing one jot of the natural folly of a monkey."

22 Wells to Rebecca, early August 1928.
23 Wells to Rebecca, fall? 1928.
24 Wells to Rebecca, fall? 1928.
25 Wells to Rebecca, 16 September 1928.
26 Wells to Rebecca, 19 December 1928.
27 Theobald Mathew to Rebecca, 15 January 1929.
28 Theobald Mathew to Rebecca, 13 and 18 March 1929.
29 Wells to Rebecca, 29 April 1929.
30 Theobald Mathew to Rebecca, 24 June 1929.
31 Rebecca to Theobald Mathew, 23 July 1929.
32 Rebecca to Anthony West, 23 July 1929.
33 Rebecca to Theobald Mathew, 11 September 1929.
34 Rebecca to Bertrand Russell, early September 1929.
35 Wells to Rebecca, 13 September 1929.
36 Wells to Rebecca, 8 January 1930.
37 Wells to Rebecca, 9 March 1930.
38 Wells to Rebecca, 21 March 1930.
39 W. Gedge Fiske to Theobald Mathew, 18 March 1930.
40 Rebecca, statement of 1944 (Ray).
41 Rebecca to Wells, 2 January 1932. There are virtually no letters of the sort described by Dame Rebecca among those that I have seen. Since they were in Mathew's custody at one point, they may have remained with Messrs. Charles Russell and have been destroyed when that firm moved its premises after the war. They could also be among Dame Rebecca's inaccessible papers.
42 Rebecca to S. K. Ratcliffe, 30 October 1930 (Yale).
43 Theobald Mathew to Rebecca, 13 February 1931.

44 Wells to Rebecca, 13 October 1934. It should be mentioned that Rebecca knew nothing of these articles, which were published while she and her husband were travelling abroad.
45 Wells to Rebecca, 14 January 1935.
46 Wells to Rebecca, 5 March 1935.
47 Rebecca, statement of 1957 (Ray). Members of Wells's family recall that breakfast was his only substantial meal during his last years.
48 Rebecca to Marjorie Wells, 21 August 1946 (G. P. Wells).

GENERAL INDEX

Abbotsford, 85
Adams, Franklin P., 155
Alderton, xvii, 66–71, 74–75, 77, 199
Alexander the Great, 93
Andrews, Henry Maxwell, 190, 192, 193
Arlen, Michael, 151
Ashford, Daisy, *The Young Visiters*, 96
Asquith, Herbert Henry, 12, 27, 30
Astor, Lady, 142
Aumonier, Stacey, 151

Barnes, Kenneth, 6
Bax, Belfort, *The Fraud of Feminism*, 28
Beaverbrook, Max (Lord Beaverbrook), 141
Beinecke Library, Yale University, 195
Belloc Lowndes, Marie, 110
Benckendorf, Moura, 103
Bennett, Arnold, 169, 175, 182
Bercovici, Konrad, 157
Bland, Mrs. Hubert, xxv
Blatchford, Robert, 15, 38
Bottomley, Horatio, 23
Braughing, Hertfordshire, xvii, 58, 60–66, 125, 199
Brett, George Platt, 110
Broun, Heywood, 156
Bryant, Major, 168, 170

Buddha, 93
Byron, George Gordon, Lord, xxii

Campbell, Joan, 117
Chekov, Anton, *The Seagull,* 19
Chesterton, G. K., 27, 31
Chicago Tribune, 113
Clarion, 15, 16, 27, 28–31, 35, 38, 41–42, 196, 197, 198, 199
Clausen, Mr. Justice, 181–182
Claverton Street rooms, 75–76, 77, 125, 201
Collins, Wilkie, xx
Conrad, Joseph, 179
Cosmos Club, Washington, 113, 114
Craye, Mr., 177

Daily Express, 140
Daily Herald, 140
Daily Mail, 12
Daily News, 51, 62, 63, 69, 140, 177
Dansey, Pat, 117
Deslys, Gaby, 38, 41
Dickens, Charles, 81
Duchinsky, Frau, 135, 142
Duchinsky, Herr, 136, 142

Easton Glebe. *See* Little Easton Rectory
"Elizabeth." *See* Russell, Countess

PRINCIPAL FIGURES INDEX

WORKS BY H. G. WELLS